VIKING SOCIETY FOR NORTHERN RESEARCH
TEXT SERIES

GENERAL EDITORS

Anthony Faulkes and Alison Finlay

VOLUME XVII

CLEMENS SAGA

THE LIFE OF ST CLEMENT OF ROME

CLEMENS SAGA

THE LIFE OF ST CLEMENT OF ROME

EDITED AND TRANSLATED

BY

HELEN CARRON

VIKING SOCIETY FOR NORTHERN RESEARCH
UNIVERSITY COLLEGE LONDON
2005

ISBN: 0 903521 67 9

Printed by Short Run Press Limited, Exeter

CONTENTS

ACKNOWLEDGMENTS

This edition originated from the work done for my University of London PhD thesis (1994) under the supervision of Peter Foote. I wish to thank Anthony Faulkes and Peter Foote for their generous advice and help with this edition, and also Alison Finlay for reading through the final version.

H. C. C.

INTRODUCTION

I *Saints' lives in Iceland*

St Clement (fl. c. 96), known as Clement of Rome, was bishop of Rome, generally considered to be third in the line of succession from St Peter after Linus and Cletus. His feast-day is the twenty-third of November. His life, *Clemens saga*, is among the earliest saints' lives translated into Icelandic.

Iceland was converted to Christianity at the beginning of the eleventh century. In this period the first saints' lives, initially in Latin, and some Norwegian translations of Latin texts, would have reached Iceland. To make the lives available to a wider audience than the educated clergy they were translated into the vernacular. This is thought to have taken place in the course of the twelfth century. The earliest surviving Icelandic manuscripts of vernacular saints' lives date from the beginning of the thirteenth century, whereas the earliest extant Norwegian manuscripts date from the end of the twelfth century. For example fragments of three translated saints' lives, *Blasíus saga*, *Mattheus saga* and *Plácidus saga*, are found in AM 655 IX 4to, which is considered to have been written c. 1150–1200 (Ólafur Halldórsson 1994, lxv; *Ordbog* 1989, 459), and thought by some scholars to be the oldest surviving Norwegian manuscript. Some early Norwegian manuscripts of saints' lives may have soon found their way to Iceland.

It is to this genre of literature known as saints' lives (in Icelandic *Heilagra manna sögur*) that *Clemens saga* belongs. Saints' lives are biographies of holy men and women. They were initially written in the language of the Church, Latin, and when the need arose they were subsequently translated into the vernaculars. Translated saints' lives are thought to have been among the earliest sagas written in Iceland. In a well-known passage in *Origins of Icelandic literature* Gabriel Turville-Petre (1953, 142) put forward the view that saints' lives influenced native written literature: 'In a word, the learned literature did not teach the Icelanders what to think or what to say, but it taught them how to say it.' This has been the subject of much debate. In a paper entitled 'Saints' lives and sagas' Peter Foote (1994, 73–88) took Gabriel Turville-Petre's statement as his main theme, considered it and suggested the following revised version: 'The learned literature by no means dictated the Icelanders' choice and treatment of subject matter, of what they said; but it taught them something about how to say it—also, about how not to say it'. It is difficult to substantiate what influence this genre of literature may have had on native saga writing, but it is unlikely that it would have been entirely without influence.

One area in which learned or religious texts like *Clemens saga* may
have had some influence on other saga writing is in their depiction of the
character of the 'noble heathen'. For instance parallels can be drawn
between the concept of the 'noble heathen' as described by Lars Lönnroth
(1969, 1–29) and the characters of Faustinianus and his son Clement and
other members of his family as portrayed in *Clemens saga*. The 'noble
heathen' is a pagan hero whose nobility is innate and causes him or her to
act in a manner one would expect of a Christian hero. Lönnroth draws
examples of this concept from *Vatnsdœla saga*, e.g. the heathen Þorsteinn
invokes the 'creator of the sun' and makes a promise to take care of a
child who was left out to die in return for the healing of his brother Þórir
(*ÍF* VIII, 97–98). The 'noble heathen' is both wise and virtuous. This is
true of Clement's father, Faustinianus. Faustinianus is wise, and is said to
have followed Roman custom by worshipping carven images, but not
wholeheartedly because he believed in the existence of one God (*Clemens
saga* Ch. 2). He prays to the one God for guidance (Ch. 4). His wife
Mathidia is highly virtuous, and in a similar way to Þorsteinn she invokes
a sun-god, the pagan god Apollo (Ch. 2). Before he is converted to
Christianity Clement reveals his inherent nobility by his generous reception
of the Apostle Barnabas in Rome (Ch. 5).

According to Lönnroth the 'noble heathen' was an attempt to solve the
dilemma of reconciling pagan tradition with the teachings of the church.
He believes that it is possible that this concept was known very early to
Icelanders through foreign literature, i.e. learned literature, as well as
through theological doctrine. In support of this he refers to *Plácidus saga*
(Life of St Eustace), the story of which shares similarities with that of St
Clement (see Section II.1 below). Examples of Lönnroth's concept can
be found in Ch. VII of *Clemens saga*, which tells of Clement's teaching,
his attempts to convert the heathen, and his subsequent exile and
martyrdom. Here an attempt is made to reconcile the differences between
other faiths and Clement's teaching. This is done by placing emphasis on
the affection which both heathen men and Jews had for Clement. The
point is made that Clement did not ridicule pagan religion, but tried to
convert men to Christianity through rational arguments based on their
own books. Through his methods many heathens were converted to
Christianity, but this aroused the jealousy of a heathen named Publius
Torquatianus, who incited discord and caused Clement to be accused of
blaspheming the pagan gods, which resulted in his exile and martyrdom.

Martyrium S. Clementis (*PG* 2, cols 625–26) names nine pagan gods
whom Clement is said to have blasphemed: Jove, Hercules, Venus, Vesta,

Minerva, Diana, Mercury, Saturn and Mars. The author of *Clemens saga* translates the names of these gods into their Icelandic equivalents for his readers, for example Jove/Jupiter becomes Þórr, Hercules becomes Óðinn. He lists fourteen gods in all: Þórr, Óðinn, Freyja, Freyr, Heimdallr, Loki, Hœnir, Baldr, Týr, Njǫrðr, Ullr, Frigg, Gefjun and Sif (see Section III below).

It is significant that there is no criticism of the heathens Clement converts, or of their former religion. The Prefect of Rome, Mamertus Julianus, who sends Clement into exile, is also portrayed as a 'noble heathen'. He is moved by Clement's declaration of his Christian faith, and blesses his journey into exile (*Clemens saga* Ch. 8). (On the subject of pagan sympathy see Faulkes 1983, 283–314.)

Within the genre of saints' lives in Icelandic there are different categories: lives of the Apostles, lives of holy men and holy women who were martyred for their faith, lives of confessors (*ODCC* 330: men or women who suffered for confessing their faith, but who were not martyred, e.g. St Martin of Tours, see *Heilagra manna søgur* 1877, I 554–74), lives of Fathers of the Church (*ODCC* 504: ecclesiastical authors of the past whose authority on doctrinal matters carried weight, e.g. St Ambrose, Bishop of Milan (c. 339–97; *ODCC* 42–43), and also Desert Fathers, e.g. St Anthony of Egypt (251?–356; *ODCC* 67–68); and lives of native saints, e.g. the life of the first Bishop of Hólar, Jón Ǫgmundarson (1106–21), *Jóns saga ins helga* (*ÍF* XV:2, 173–316; trans. Cormack 2000, 595–626).

Clemens saga fits into the second category, a life of a devout man who was martyred for his faith. St Clement met his death by drowning; he was pushed overboard from a boat with an anchor tied around his neck.

Saints' lives generally follow a defined structure which is composed of certain elements. The life of a saint who was martyred because of his or her faith is as a rule divided into three parts: the life itself, the martyrdom, and the saint's influence after death. The last includes miracles associated with the saint. In *Clemens saga* the saint's martyrdom is followed by the story of the miracle of the child who was left behind near the saint's coffin in the church under the sea and was discovered alive a year later. Among the elements commonly found in saints' lives are accounts of the saint's virtues, his or her conversion to Christianity, the testing of his or her faith by trials and tribulations and the miraculous state of his or her corpse after death. But *Clemens saga* is not typical. Although there is some account of Clement's early life before his conversion, it is sketchy, and instead the narrative is focused on the lives of members of his family and their trials and tribulations before they were converted to Christianity by St Peter.

Special emphasis is placed on the virtues of Clement's mother. Clement does not undergo any trials or tribulations relating to his faith until he approaches his martyrdom.

The number of manuscripts containing saints' lives which have survived attests to the popularity of this genre. Biographies of saints played an important role in the liturgy of the medieval Church. Extracts from them were included in Church service books, and lives might be read out on the appropriate saint's Feast Day in daily services or read as part of personal devotions. The lives extolled the virtues of a holy life. Veneration of the saints was a part of daily life, and both men and women had favourite saints to whom they would pray and whom they would ask to intercede on their behalf. Sturla Þórðarson's favourite saint was said to be the Apostle St Peter (*Sturlunga saga* 1946, II 236). The miracle of wounds which did not bleed was a powerful motif in saints' lives and was adopted from them into secular literature. It is used in *Svínfellinga saga*, one of the texts included in the compilation known as *Sturlunga saga*. After his description of the execution of Sæmundr Ormsson, the saga author notes that Sæmundr's corpse did not bleed (*Sturlunga saga* 1946, II 100). Similarly, in saints' lives, although a saint might be martyred by torture, his or her body would often remain unblemished. In *Njáls saga* Njáll is almost regarded as a saint when his face and body, after the burning of his homestead, are described by one of those who discovered him as *svá bjartr, at ek hefi engan dauðs manns líkama sét jafnbjartan*, 'so bright that I have seen no dead person's body as bright' (*ÍF* XII 343).

Two saga heroes, Þorgils skarði and Hrafn Sveinbjarnarson, each choose to hear a saint's life read out aloud to them on the evenings before they meet their deaths. Þorgils skarði stays at a homestead at Hrafnagil overnight. From the various forms of entertainment offered to him during the evening he chooses to hear the life of St Thomas Becket. It is read out aloud to the assembled company, up to the point where Thomas was murdered in Canterbury Cathedral. In the night Þorgils is betrayed, and his enemies are admitted to the building in which he is sleeping. Þorgils is murdered, and one of the wounds he is said to have received is on the head, and thus similar to that suffered by St Thomas (*Sturlunga saga* 1946, II 218, 220–21). In *Hrafns saga Sveinbjarnarsonar* (1987, 41) Hrafn is unable to sleep the night before his death, and asks a man named Steingrímr to recite *Andreasdrápa*, a poem the surviving fragment of which is largely about the martyrdom of St Andrew.

Clemens saga tells the story of the life of Clement of Rome, how he and his family are converted to Christianity and become disciples of St Peter, then how he succeeds St Peter as bishop of Rome, his subsequent martyrdom, and miracles associated with him before and after his martyrdom. The story is mainly told in the third person. It divides neatly into two sections, the first dealing with St Clement and his family, the second dealing with his martyrdom. The first section is ultimately derived from the text known as the *Recognitiones* (see Section II.1 below), the second from a Latin *Passio* (see Section II.2 below).

II.1 *Material from the Recognitiones*

The first section of *Clemens saga* is derived from the text known as the *Recognitiones* (Rehm 1965; translated in *The Ante-Nicene Fathers* 8 (1995), 75–211), one of the writings attributed to Clement of Rome which are now acknowledged not to be by him but to have had their origin in the fourth century. These writings, the so-called Pseudo-Clementines, survive in three forms: the *Recognitiones*, homilies, and epitomes. The homilies were written in Greek, the epitomes are extant in Greek and Arabic. The *Recognitiones* were translated from Greek into Latin by Tyrannius Rufinus (c. 345–410), presbyter of Aquileia, who was responsible for translating many Greek theological works into Latin (*ODCC* 1207–08). The name *Recognitiones* is derived from the scenes of recognition between Clement and the long-lost members of his family. The story is similar to that of the life of St Eustace. Both Eustace and Clement are separated from their families and believe them to be dead, and then a series of recognitions take place in which the family members recognise each other and are joyfully reunited. Eustace's wife, like Clement's mother Mathidia, is virtuous and upright and undergoes various tribulations before she is reunited with her husband and sons. Versions of the life of St Eustace are extant in Icelandic in both prose and verse, namely *Plácidus saga* and *Plácidus drápa*. The earliest manuscript of *Plácidus saga*, one fragmentary leaf in AM 655 IX 4to, is considered to have been written between 1150 and 1200, possibly in Trondheim (*Plácidus saga* 1998, lx). The verse life of St Eustace, *Plácidus drápa,* is in AM 673b 4to, dated c. 1200. In his edition of *Plácidus saga* (1988, xxi), John Tucker mentioned the possibility that the Clementine romance, i.e. the story of Clement and his family, may have served as the model for the writing of the Eustace legend.

The popularity of the story of St Clement and his family is attested by the number of lives of St Clement which were derived and adapted from the *Recognitiones* from the sixth century onwards. Among them, for example, is a sixth-century Latin work known as *Historia Certaminis*

Apostolici (Pseudo-Abdias 1560), derived from a work attributed to the fictional author, Abdias of Babylon, said to have been the first bishop of Babylon, appointed by St Simon and St Jude and among the seventy-two disciples of Christ. *Historia Certaminis Apostolici* was attributed to Abdias by W. Lazius in 1552. The work is now considered to have been compiled from earlier sources by two anonymous authors in sixth-century Gaul (*New Catholic Encyclopedia* 2003, I 13–14). It contains Clementine material derived from the *Recognitiones* and a *Passio*. This text was used in the fifteenth century by Boninus Mombritius in his *Sanctuarium seu vitae sanctorum*, c. 1480 (Mombritius 1978), and it was also used by Johann Albert Fabricius in his *Codex Apocryphus Novi Testamenti*, 1703–19.

In his work *Die Legende von Sankt Clemens in den skandinavischen Ländern im Mittelalter* (1997) Dietrich Hofmann identified a number of Latin lives of St Clement. The oldest of them, entitled *Vita sancti Clementis*, is that by Johannes Diaconus Hymmonides and Bishop Gaudericus of Velletri (1968, 1–164; see Hofmann 1997, 18). It was written in the ninth century between 876 and 882 and dedicated by Gaudericus to Pope John VIII (872–82). This life has partially survived in an eleventh-century manuscript from Monte Cassino. The manuscript is defective and the second part, containing the end of *Vita sancti Clementis*, is lost. About the beginning of the twelfth century Leo Marsicanus (c. 1045–c. 1116), monk of Monte Cassino, and Gaudericus's successor as cardinal bishop of Ostia and Velletri, appears to have edited part of the *Vita sancti Clementis* (Hofmann 1997, 19). Leo's work is known by the title *De origine beati Clementis* (Johannes Diaconus Hymmonides and Bishop Gaudericus of Velletri 1968, 1–165, parallel with *Vita sancti Clementis*). Both these Latin lives stem from Rufinus's version of the *Recognitiones*.

In the twelfth century Honorius of Autun included the story of St Clement in *Speculum Ecclesiae* (*PL* 172, cols 1029–32), and in the next century Vincent of Beauvais (c. 1190–1264) in his encyclopaedic work, *Speculum Historiale* (Book 9, Chs 23–37; Book 10, Chs 52–54; in *Speculum Maius* 4, 1591), included excerpts from the life of St Clement extracted from both the *Recognitiones* and the *Passio*. There is also a life of St Clement to be found in verse in the South English Legendary, the earliest version of which is thought to date from the late thirteenth century (*Cambridge History of Medieval English Literature* 1999, 619). In the *Legenda Aurea* compiled by Jacob of Voragine c. 1255–66 there is a life of St Clement which is closer to the *Recognitiones* than to the Icelandic version (Jacobus de Voragine 1890, 777–88 and 1993, II 323–32). Mathias Tveitane (1985, 1069) thought that although the *Legenda Aurea* itself could not be a direct source of the Icelandic version (it is too late), some connection between the source of the *Legenda Aurea* and the source of the Icelandic was conceivable.

Episodes from the story of St Clement which derive from the *Recognitiones* are also found in two redactions of the life of St Peter the Apostle, *Pétrs saga postola* I (*Postola sögur* 1874, 1–126) and *Pétrs saga postola* II (*Postola sögur* 1874, 159–201).

Pétrs saga II is thought to have been compiled in the twelfth century. This version was part of the thirteenth century codex AM 652 4to. Unfortunately AM 652 4to has only survived fragmentarily and none of the extant fragments are from *Pétrs saga*. For the full text of *Pétrs saga* II one has to rely on copies of AM 652 4to which were made in the seventeenth century when the codex was still complete, namely AM 630 4to and AM 659 a 4to. It was the former, AM 630 4to, which Unger used in his edition (designated *Pétrs saga* IIA). The text relating to St Clement is printed on pp. 172–79. A recension of *Pétrs saga* II is included fragmentarily in AM 645 4to (*Postola sögur* 1874, 201–11; Larsson 1885; for the text relating to *Clemens saga* see *Postola sögur* 1874, 203), which also contains *Clemens saga*. The fragment in AM 655 XII–XIII 4to (*Pétrs saga* IIB, *Postola sögur* 1874, 211–16) contains no Clementine material. *Pétrs saga* I is a younger redaction, probably compiled in the fourteenth century from various Latin sources, and is extant in three fourteenth-century manuscripts, Codex Scardensis (SÁM I), Stockholm perg. 19 4to and AM 239 4to (defective).

Pétrs saga IIA (AM 630 4to) shares only two episodes from the life of St Clement with *Clemens saga* and *Pétrs saga* I, the dispute between St Peter and Simon Magus in Caesarea and St Peter's meeting with Clement's mother. Only the latter has survived in AM 645 4to.

Of the two redactions of *Pétrs saga*, the account in *Pétrs saga* I of St Clement is the more comparable with that of *Clemens saga*. It tells the story of Clement and his family but does not include his martyrdom.

Various differences are to be found between the texts of *Clemens saga* and the two redactions of *Pétrs saga*. In *Pétrs saga* I Clement's story is arranged in a different order to that of *Clemens saga*. In *Clemens saga* the account begins with an introduction which sets the scene with Clement's family background, the story of his father, mother and uncle. This is then followed directly by the tale of Niceta, Aquila and Mathidia's shipwreck, and then Faustinianus's reception of the news. In contrast *Pétrs saga* I places Faustinianus's story at the time of his dispute with Clement in the presence of St Peter. The scene of recognition after this is followed in turn by Mathidia's story and likewise that of her two sons, Clement's brothers, Niceta and Aquila (Faustus and Faustinus). In *Clemens saga* the account is mainly in the third person, but *Pétrs saga* I makes use of the first person, each character in turn, Faustinianus, Mathidia, Niceta and Aquila (Faustus and Faustinus), relating the misfortunes which befell him or her.

Among the other differences between the texts the following details in *Clemens saga* can be noted which are not found in the equivalent text of *Pétrs saga* I: in *Clemens saga* it is stated that Simon Magus was reared for ten years by Rakel, that he gave life to images made from wood or metal, and that he was able to change his form to that of a bird, snake, fish, deer etc., whereas in *Pétrs saga* I only two forms, sheep and goat, are identified.

There are also differences between the two texts in the introductory description of Simon Magus. In *Clemens saga* he claims that he is the sun, his mistress/wife the moon and the planets her handmaidens, and comments are added on the Latin words for the moon and the planets. There are no such comments in *Pétrs saga* I, and Simon's consort is described as a harlot from Tyre.

In the episode in which Clement's mother, Mathidia, arrives at the house of a female leper there is variation between the two saga texts. In *Pétrs saga* I the leper asks Mathidia why she has come to her house, and Mathidia answers. This is lacking in *Clemens saga*, but this could possibly be due to omission by a copyist.

The dispute between St Peter and Simon Magus is contained in Books II and III of the *Recognitiones*. The versions in *Clemens saga* and *Pétrs saga* are shortened. Moreover in comparison with both *Pétrs saga* I and II *Clemens saga* provides a severely abbreviated version of the dialogue between St Peter and Simon Magus. Peter's opening address beginning 'Let there be peace to all who are ready to believe the truth' takes up approximately twenty-seven lines in Unger's edition of *Pétrs saga* I (twenty-two lines in *Pétrs saga* II), but in *Clemens saga* this is reduced to a single line. Also Simon's reply to St Peter, twelve lines in *Pétrs saga* I (sixteen lines in *Pétrs saga* II), consists only of one sentence in *Clemens saga*, 'We don't need to accept peace from you'.

Moreover there are differences between the text in *Pétrs saga* II of the dispute between St Peter and Simon Magus and that to be found in *Pétrs saga* I and *Clemens saga*. In *Pétrs saga* II Zacheus is described as a leader of the city, not a bishop. In the *Pétrs saga* II text the reference to Simon having been given a sickle by his mother and sent to reap the corn is placed at the end of his list of skills, whereas in *Pétrs saga* I and *Clemens saga* it is at the beginning. *Pétrs saga* II also does not mention that he was seen flying up into the air at the end of the dispute episode, whereas this is noted in both *Pétrs saga* I and *Clemens saga* (*Postola sögur* 1874, 53/7, *Clemens saga* 18/3–4).

There are also differences in detail between the accounts of the same episode in *Clemens saga* and *Pétrs saga* I. At the end of the dispute *Clemens saga* alone notes that 'night fell and it began to get dark when Simon vanished'. In the same episode *Clemens saga* states that when St Peter and Simon Magus held their dispute Clement attended the meeting with a large following. At the corresponding point in the text of *Pétrs saga* I there is no reference to Clement's presence. In *Pétrs saga* I it is stated that before the dispute, St Peter sent away men who had not been baptised, but those who had received baptism accompanied him to the meeting. Both sagas agree in relating that Clement was not baptised until after the dispute.

The other episode found in *Clemens saga* and shared by *Pétrs saga* I and II is that of St Peter's meeting with Clement's mother (the AM 645 4to text (*Postola sögur* 203) is more or less identical to that of *Pétrs saga* IIA (*Postola sögur* 179)). According to *Pétrs saga* IIA Peter lands on the island of Antaradus. Here there is confusion in the text between the island named Aradus and Antaradus on the mainland. St Peter is said to have come to a house in which he sees pillars made of glass and where he discovers a woman, Clement's mother, begging for alms outside. The woman's mistress is said to be paralytic. The version of the story related in *Clemens saga* and *Pétrs saga* I is different; in that version the island is Corfu, not Aradus or Antaradus, there is no house with glass pillars, Clement's mother is said to have gone to meet St Peter herself, and her mistress is said to be suffering from leprosy.

There is one episode, the story of Simon Magus's ex-disciple Marcellus and St Peter, which is present in the two redactions of *Pétrs saga* but omitted in *Clemens saga*. The story derives from the *Recognitiones*, but in the Latin text Simon's disciple is unnamed, whereas in *Pétrs saga* he is named Marcellus. This is probably traditionally linked with the *Pseudo-Marcellus Passio* (Lipsius 1959, 118–77) which is one of the sources used in both redactions of *Pétrs saga*. It might be supposed that the omission of this episode in *Clemens saga* was because it was not directly relevant to the story of St Clement.

As well as differences between the Icelandic texts containing material relating to St Clement there are also significant differences between the Icelandic texts and their ultimate Latin source, the *Recognitiones*. The most obvious difference between the Icelandic and Latin texts is in length. Mattias Tveitane drew attention to the length of the *Recognitiones* compared to the shorter text in *Clemens saga* (Tveitane 1985, 1069). Comparison between the Icelandic Clementine material and Rufinus's Latin translation of the *Recognitiones* shows that the Icelandic version is much shorter and related only to the bare bones of the *Recognitiones*. The lengthy theological and philosophical discussions of the *Recognitiones* are not included in the Icelandic texts.

Another main difference is that the Latin text is autobiographical— Clement tells his story in the first person—whereas the Icelandic accounts are mainly related in the third person.

Among other significant differences between the Icelandic and Latin texts the following can be noted. The version of the tale of Clement's mother, Mathidia, being shipwrecked off the island of Corfu in *Clemens saga* and *Pétrs saga* I, does not correspond to the text of the *Recognitiones*, where Mathidia is wrecked off an island named Aradus (Andaradus in *Pétrs saga postola* II; *Postola sögur* 1874, 179 and 203), and is given shelter by a poor woman who has lost her husband at sea. The woman becomes paralytic and Mathidia is forced to beg. The remainder of Mathidia's story in the *Recognitiones* corresponds to that in *Pétrs saga* II in which St Peter encounters Mathidia begging at the doors of a house. Both texts describe a building with columns. In the *Recognitiones* the building is a temple with *columnas viteas*, 'columns carved with vines', and in *Pétrs saga* II it is a house with columns made of glass, which correspond to the *columnas vitreas* of the Latin texts of Mombritius and Fabricius. In *Clemens saga* and *Pétrs saga* I Mathidia's story is very different from the Latin and the account in *Pétrs saga* II, and emphasises Mathidia's virtue. In these two accounts Mathidia is first taken in by a housewife after the shipwreck, given lodging and in return works as a seamstress, making and mending clothes. She becomes the unwilling object of attention from the young men who see her and admire her handiwork and beauty. As a result Mathidia mars her face by beating it with sharp stones and then covers her face with a fish skin to make her appearance repugnant. She also injures her hands so that she can no longer work. Eventually she has to leave her lodgings, is offered a home by a poor woman, and resorts to begging to support them both. This account appears to be peculiar to the Icelandic version.

The account of the dispute between Clement and his father Faustinianus differs in the Icelandic from the Latin. In the Icelandic St Peter first encounters Clement's father, Faustinianus, near a cliff on Cyprus. In the Latin St Peter, Clement and his brothers Niceta and Aquila bathe in the sea at Laodocia, then go to a secret place to pray and there they meet Faustinianus.

The Icelandic text turns the dispute with Faustinianus into one based on the seven liberal arts with Clement as Faustinianus's sole antagonist, whereas in the *Recognitiones* it is described as a philosophical dispute with Faustinianus which is carried on over several days and in which all three of Faustinianus's sons take part.

The version in *Clemens saga* and *Pétrs saga* I of the episode in which Clement's father Faustinianus encounters Simon Magus in Antioch also differs from the Latin. In the *Recognitiones* Faustinianus's friends in Antioch are named Appion and Anubion, but the Icelandic names one friend only, who is called Theophilus, and later reference is made to the consecration as a church by St Peter of a hall owned by Theophilus. In the Icelandic version the story appears to have been simplified by transferring Theophilus to the role of Faustinianus's friend. The Icelandic version also includes additional details which are not in the Latin, namely that St Peter advised Faustinianus to have two men ready to hold a shield in front of him for protection when he addressed the crowd in Antioch, and that when this came to pass Simon Magus had arrows shot at Faustinianus, who was protected by his shield.

There are other minor differences between the Icelandic and Latin texts. Faustinianus's brother is not named in the Latin text, but in the Icelandic he is called Bassus. In the reign of Nero there was a consul called Bassus, and this may possibly be the source of the name (see Cullmann 1962, 124). Clement's brothers, Niceta and Aquila, are twins according to the *Recognitiones*, but they are not described as such in the Icelandic text.

From the above comparison of *Clemens saga* and the two redactions of *Pétrs saga* the following can be established. The variants identified in the *Pétrs saga* II text are peculiar to the type of Latin text which are found in editions of the text called the *Historia Certaminis Apostolici*, attributed to Abdias of Babylon (see pp. xi–xii above). Moreover it may be noted that after the Clementine material both *Pétrs saga* II and the Abdias text relate the story of how St Peter cured a girl who was mad. This is not present in either *Clemens saga* or *Pétrs saga* I. It may also be observed that the *Pétrs saga* II version and that of Abdias share the peculiarity that neither text names Clement's mother.

The points shared by the *Pétrs saga* II text and Abdias's text indicate that the *Pétrs saga* II text is derived from a similar Latin text, of a type identified by Mattias Tveitane (1985, 1073) as an epitome with the traditional title *Virtutes Petri*, and an Incipit 'Surrexit quidam Simon Magus'. The details of St Peter's encounter with Clement's mother are closer to the *Recognitiones* than to the accounts in *Clemens saga* and

Pétrs saga I (see p. xvi above), and this shows that the text of *Pétrs saga* II had a different derivation, and provides evidence for the existence of two vernacular versions of part of the Clementine material in early thirteenth-century Iceland.

Clemens saga and *Pétrs saga* I tell the same version of the story of Clement and his family, the ultimate source of which is the *Recognitiones*. *Clemens saga* is not abridged save in the shortening of the dispute episode and the omission of the Marcellus episode, the latter superfluous to a life of St Clement. The comparison of the Clementine material in *Clemens saga* and *Pétrs saga* I indicates that both texts were ultimately derived from the same Latin source, which was based on a free adaptation of the *Recognitiones*, but were independently translated, and the material organised according to each compiler's needs. This Latin source is likely to have been compiled in the twelfth century.[1]

II.2 *Material from the Latin Passio*

The second section of the saga deals with events leading up to and including the martyrdom of St Clement, plus a miracle which takes place after his death. The first part tells the story of a Christian woman named Theodora and her pagan husband Sisinnius. Sisinnius is converted to Christianity through the intervention of Pope Clement. Then follows the tale of Clement's exile, the miracle of the spring, his martyrdom when he is thrown overboard with an anchor tied round his neck, the miracle of his temple under the sea, and that of the child who falls asleep near the saint's coffin and is found alive there a year later.

The second section of *Clemens saga* is based on a Latin *Passio*. The tale of the miracle of St Clement's coffin under the sea was probably

---

[1] The above discussion is largely based on my unpublished thesis (Carron [1994]), and partly on the work of Dietrich Hofmann (1997, 72–108), who thought that a text similar to that found in Trinity College Oxford MS 60 was a source of *Clemens saga*, and that such a text was also the source of Johannes and Gaudericus's *Vita sancti Clementis*, which the author turned to for at least the end of the *Recognitiones* section of his saga (Hofmann 1997, 102). According to Widding 1963, 330, Chs 50–58 and 60–73 of *Pétrs saga* I are derived from a text of *Clemens saga*. In the same section of his work (1997, 72–108), Hofmann also discusses the differences to be found in the Icelandic text and possible reasons for them, and among other things raises the possibility that the compiler of *Clemens saga* had read the *Recognitiones* but did not recall all the details of the story well when he came to write *Clemens saga*. He also suggests the possibility of an oral tradition in which the story was passed down by word of mouth.

ultimately derived from the Greek text attributed to an imaginary Bishop Ephraim of Cherson which has the Latin title *De miraculo quod in puero factum est a S. Clemente sacro martyre* (printed in parallel Greek and Latin in *PG* 2, cols 633–46). Linking the sections derived from the *Recognitiones* and the *Passio* in *Clemens saga* there is a brief account of how St Peter installed Clement as his successor as bishop of Rome. This is ultimately derived from *Epistula Clementis ad Iacobum* (Rehm 1965, 375–87; translated in *The Ante-Nicene Fathers* 8 (1995), 218–22; *BHL* 6646; cf. p. 35, footnote, below), probably via an intermediate source. Hofmann (1997, 109) thought that the 'book' referred to in *Clemens saga* 34/10 could not have been the *Epistula* itself, for if it had been the compiler would have called it 'letter' rather than 'book'.

Clemens saga is defective at the end, so the miracle of the sleeping child is incomplete. The text ends abruptly at the point where the parents of the child who fell asleep near the saint's coffin ask their son how he was able to survive so long without food. The end of the miracle story, from the point where *Clemens saga* breaks off, is shorter in the *Epitome de gestis S. Petri* Chs 178–79 (*PG* 2, cols 602-03) than in the Ephraim text Chs 12–18 (*PG* 2, cols 642–46). Since *Clemens saga* is not a close translation of either text it is not possible to establish what form the ending would have taken in *Clemens saga*. In the *Epitome* the parents ask their son how he was saved, protected, watched over and his life preserved. He answers them telling them that there was a protector, bestower of life and nourisher in the church. His parents rejoice and quote Psalm 67:36 *Mirabilis Deus in sanctis suis*, 68:35 'O God ⟨thou art⟩ terrible out of thy holy places'.

It also looks as though the beginning of the miracle story has been omitted in *Clemens saga*, possibly through an error in copying. The first mention of the child and his parents is at the point when the parents realise that their son is missing. In the Epitome a devout man, his wife and son accompany others to St Clement's burial place. They reach the temple, leading the boy by the hand. The parents pray fervently inside while the boy is out of sight, and he is then forgotten and left behind at the burial place.

The *Passio* was ultimately derived from the work of the Byzantine hagiographer Simeon Metaphrastes (fl. c. 960), who compiled a collection of saints' lives known as the 'Menologion'. A parallel Greek and Latin text is printed in Cotelerius 1672, I 828–44, with Metaphrastes identified as the source. This text contains the story of Theodora and her husband Sisinnius and the exile and martyrdom of St Clement. Although reference is made in the text to the miracle of the sea receding and revealing the marble temple with the saint's coffin, the miracle of the sleeping child left in St Clement's temple is not related. Cotelerius's text was reprinted in *PG* 2 (1857), cols 617–32, and an edition of the *Passio* was published by F. X. Funk (1901, 28–45; revised edition by F. Diekamp 1913).

The Icelandic text combines the *Passio* and the miracle of the child who fell asleep in St Clement's temple. The source of this is likely to be an epitome similar to the two Greek epitomes of the *Recognitiones*, which add to their accounts of Clement's martyrdom the miracles of his temple under the sea and the sleeping child (*PG* 2, cols 469–604).

A version of the life of St Clement in an Old Swedish Legendary, which is based on the *Recognitiones*, similarly combines its text of the *Passio* with the miracle of the sleeping child (Hofmann 1997, 305–21). The Life of St Clement in Jacob of Voragine's *Legenda Aurea* (c. 1255–66) also includes the story of the temple under the sea and the miracle of the sleeping child, and the story is similar to that in Gregory of Tours, *De Gloria martyrium* (*Glory of the Martyrs*), i.e. a woman leaves her son behind by St Clement's church/temple, the sea covers the temple/church, and a year later when the sea recedes the woman returns and finds her son asleep where she left him.

Gregory became Bishop of Tours in 573. He is considered to have written his work on the martyrs towards the end of his life (Gregory of Tours 1988, 4). There are differences between the text attributed to Ephraim and that of Gregory (see Hofmann 1997, 137–38). Whereas both parents of the sleeping child are mentioned in the Ephraim text, the Greek epitome and *Clemens saga*, only the mother of the child is referred to in Gregory of Tours and the Old Swedish Legendary. *Clemens saga* and the Old Swedish Legendary mention that the child fell asleep at St Clement's temple, whereas Ephraim does not give this as the reason the child was left behind. In Gregory's version the child is discovered still asleep in the saint's temple a year later. A similar account based on Gregory of Tours's version is found in Ælfric's tenth-century *Natale Sancti Clementis* in his *Catholic Homilies* (Clemoes 1997, 501–02). In Ephraim and the version related in *Clemens saga* both parents return to the saint's temple, find their son alive, he runs to greet them and they rejoice.

There is no doubt that the version of this miracle in *Clemens saga* is closer to the Greek texts than to Gregory of Tours, but the Icelandic is not a direct translation of the Ephraim text. It is likely that the compiler of *Clemens saga* used a Latin translation of the Greek version, which was probably added to an epitome of the *Recognitiones*. Hofmann concluded that the author of *Clemens saga* used a Latin text which had made use of the Greek version of the miracle, and suggested that it might have been the lost part of the life of Clement by Johannes and Gaudericus (Hofmann 1997, 144).

III *Structure and Style*

The saga is divided into two sections, the story of Clement and his family and an account of Clement's martyrdom, reflecting the two main sources used by the compiler, the *Recognitiones* and the *Passio* (see section II above).

There are indications that the compiler/translator adapted his sources with his audience in mind. It is likely that he supplied the genealogical details of St Clement's family and background details of Roman history contained in the introductory chapters to the saga as a parallel to the genealogical introductions common in Sagas of Icelanders. The genealogical and historical details do not derive from either of the two main sources. Dietrich Hofmann (1997, 60–71) investigated the introductory chapters, and compared them with both *Rómverja saga* and *Veraldar saga* and concluded that the author of *Clemens saga* knew *Rómverja saga* and had used it in his introduction, but that it was uncertain whether he also knew *Veraldar saga*.

There are other indications that the saga was adapted for an Icelandic audience. Icelandic equivalents are used for the names of the Roman gods, e.g. the Temple of Jupiter (*Templum Jovis*) is translated Þórshof (2/4), Venus becomes Freyja (44/10), but the planet Venus is translated *Friggjar stjarna* (10/6) and Mars becomes Týr (44/11). Fourteen gods are listed in Ch. VII though only nine appear in the Latin sources. Not all of the Latin counterparts to the Icelandic names can be identified. Tveitane (1985) compared the names of gods in various translated Icelandic texts and established that the following equivalents were often used: Óðinn for Hercules, Gefjun for Diana/Artemis (see *Páls saga postola* I, 223/16, and *Hauksbók* 241; also for Athene/Minerva, see *Trójumanna saga* 10, and Venus, see *Stjórn* 1862, 90), Týr for Mars (e.g. *Páls saga postola* II 249/9) but Freyr and Óðinn were also identified with Mars (Óðinn also with Mercury in the name for Wednesday), and Saturn with Njǫrðr and Freyr (cf. *Trójumanna saga* 1/3–5: *var sá maðr upp fœddr í ey þeiri í Jórsalahafi er Krít heitir er Saturnus var kallaðr en vér kǫllum Frey*). Sif corresponds to Juno in *Hauksbók* and *Trójumanna saga* (also once to Thetis). The name of the god Apollo has not been changed in the text of *Clemens saga* (4/9), probably because there was no accepted Icelandic equivalent. Latin equivalents for the gods Heimdallr, Loki, Hœnir, Baldr and Ullr have not been identified. The insults in Ch. 7 are reminiscent of those in the Eddic poem *Lokasenna*, and that to Freyja of Hjalti's 'blasphemy' in *Íslendinga-bók* Ch. 7 (*ÍF* I 15).

Often the compiler/translator takes the trouble to give the Latin word corresponding to the Icelandic he uses in his text, for example he notes that the Latin noun *planeta* corresponds to his Icelandic phrase *stjǫrnur þær fimm es lausar fara í lopti* (14/16). In the disputation between Clement and his father Faustinianus in Ch. V the subjects discussed are referred to by their Latin names followed by a definition of their meaning in Icelandic. In 2/11–12 explanation is included of the derivation of the names of the two months July and August, although this could have been taken from another source; a similar treatment is found in *Veraldar saga* 1944, 49 and 50. When reference is made to the island of Cyprus a note is added to explain that it is known to Northmen by the name Kípr (10/24).

The story of Clement and his family has been adapted from the first person of its ultimate Latin source text, and told mainly in the third person, with only a few episodes being related by the characters in first-person narration. In relating the misfortunes of the various members of Clement's family the writer departs from the normal Icelandic method of strictly chronological narrative.

Among the points of style that can be noted are the following. There are abrupt transitions from indirect to direct speech, e.g. 36/29–31, 38/20–21, a phenomenon found frequently in native saga writing or the 'popular' saga style. Word pairs are used on occasion to translate a single Latin word, for example *spakr maðr ok vitr* 44/30, *illa ok herfiliga* (for the Latin *misere*) 36/7. There is alliteration in the list of pagan gods, where verbs alliterate with the name of the gods (44/9–13). The alliterating word pair *happs ok heilsu* occurs in 32/6.

In his paper 'Learned style or saga style?' (1981) Jónas Kristjánsson examined the features of learned style identified by Nygaard (1896) that occur in the oldest surviving texts of saints' lives, including *Clemens saga*. Of the examples of learned style he listed, about the only one from *Clemens saga*, and then not a distinctive one, was the use of the present participle *unnandi* in 34/27, and he concluded that this saga showed almost no characteristics of learned style. It was written before it became the fashion to rewrite and expand existing translations in the florid style, and its style is more in keeping with the 'popular' style of native sagas than with the learned style of later translated texts.

IV *Manuscripts*

Clemens saga is extant almost complete in Icelandic in only one manuscript. It is one of a number of saints' lives contained in AM 645 4to (edited in diplomatic transcript by Ludwig Larsson (1885) and in facsimile by Anne Holtsmark (1938); a normalised text of *Clemens saga* was edited by Carl Unger in *Postola sögur* 1874, 126–51 as an appendix to *Pétrs saga postola* I). AM 645 4to was written in the first half of the thirteenth century and now contains sixty-six folios, comprising two parts, an older (ff.1–42), dated c. 1220, and a later (ff. 43–66), dated c. 1225–50 (*Ordbog* 1989, 458), which were originally parts of separate manuscripts later bound together in one volume.The older section of the manuscript contains *Jarteinabók Þorláks biskups* (Book of the miracles of St Þorlákr, bishop of Skálholt 1178–93), *Clemens saga*, *Pétrs saga postola*, *Jakobs saga postola* (Life of St James the Greater), *Bartholomeus saga postola* (Life of St Bartholomew), *Mattheus saga postola* (Life of St Matthew), *Andreas saga postola* (Life of St Andrew). *Clemens saga* is on ff. 11v–24v. The later section includes a fragment of a different version of *Andreas saga* from that included in the older section, *Páls saga postola* (Life of St Paul), *Niðrstigningar saga* (Gospel of Nicodemus) and *Marteins saga biskups* (Life of St Martin of Tours).

The first three quires (ff. 1–24) are followed by a lacuna where it is believed that nine leaves have been lost (Larsson 1885, viii–x; Ólafur Halldórsson 1994, xiii). The end of *Clemens saga* and the beginning of *Pétrs saga postola* are missing.

There also survives a manuscript fragment in AM 655 XXVIII a 4to, f. 1, dated to the second half of the thirteenth century by Hreinn Benediktsson (1965, xlvi; transcription in Carron [1994]), containing the parts of the *Passio* section of *Clemens saga* corresponding to 38/27–42/34 and 44/4–50/4 in this edition. Comparison of the text of the fragment with the corresponding text of AM 645 4to reveals that the text in the fragment is shorter. For example:

En er allir svǫruþu þeir er hiá vǫru ok kvǫþu amen þá lukusk þegar upp augu Sisinnius ok eyru. (*Clemens saga* 40/2–3)

En er allir svǫruþu kvǫþu amen þá lukusk upp augu Sisinnii ok eyru. (AM 655 XXVIII a 4to f. 1r)

Cumque omnes responderunt: Amen, aperti sunt oculi Sisinnii, itemque aures. (*Martyrium S. Clementis* Ch. 9, *PG* 2, col. 622)

En þá þóttusk þrælar hans draga Clemens páfa aptr ok fram at strætum sicut Sisinnius bauþ þeim, herri þeira. En þar hlífþi Guþ heilagr Clemens páfa ástvin sínum, ok drógu þeir eptir sér of stræti stokka ok steina. Ok svá sýndisk Sisinnio sem þrælum hans at þeir drœgi þar Clemens páfa. En þeir inir sǫmu hlœgismenn es eigi vissu hvat þeir gerþu ok hlógu svá at honum sem at bandingia. En Sisinnius kvazk bana skyldu honum sem galdramǫnnum. (*Clemens saga* 40/10–17)

En þrælarnir geyrþu svá sem þeim v[a]r boðit [at] því er þeim sýndisk ok þóttusk draga Clementem páfa út ok inn. En þar drógu þeir steinsulu eina. Svá sýndisk ok Sisinnio ok hló hann at honum sem at bandingia ok kvaþsk bana mundu honum sem galdra mǫnnum. (AM 655 4to XXVIIIA 1r)

Illi vero, quos jusserat Clementem constringere ac trahere, ipsi columnas adjacentes ligabant et trahebant; aliquando quidem ex interioribus ad exteriora, aliquando vero ab exterioribus ad interiora: hoc autem ipsi etiam Sisinnio videbatur, quod sanctum Clementem ligatum tenerent ac traherent. (*Martyrium S. Clementis* Ch. 10, *PG* 2, col. 623)

AM 655 XXVIII a 4to is closer to the Latin text than AM 645 4to, translating Latin *columnas* with *steinsulu* 'stone column' and lacking the alliterating word pair *stokka oc steina* found in AM 645 4to.

It is not possible to know whether the manuscript of which this fragment was once a part also included the story of St Clement and his family or just the *Passio* section, but it provides evidence that an abridged version of this section at least existed in the later thirteenth century.

V *Date of the manuscript*

In his edition of *Mattheus saga* Ólafur Halldórsson (1994, xxvii) showed that the first part of AM 645 4to could not have been written before 1200. This dating is based on the fact that the text of *Jarteinabók Þorláks biskups*, which precedes *Clemens saga* in AM 645 4to, refers in Ch. 41 to the Alþingi (General Assembly) in the summer of 1199 at which Bishop Páll read aloud the miracles of Þorlákr and in Ch. 44 tells of a miracle which took place the second winter following Bishop Þorlákr's translation on 20 July 1198, which places this event in the winter of 1199. Ólafur qualified this dating by pointing out that Ch. 43 of the *Jarteinabók* referred to a winter mass day for Bishop Þorlákr, which implies that there already existed a summer mass day on 20 July, which according to the annals was only adopted into the law at the Alþingi of 1237. Ólafur thought it possible that both summer and winter masses could have been celebrated by churches before the summer mass became established in law, so that the date 1237 cannot be used with any certainty as the *terminus post quem*.

Ludwig Larsson (1885, lxxxvi) dated AM 645 4to between 1225 and 1250, and the orthographical features imply a date of composition in the first half of the thirteenth century. Ólafur Halldórsson supported this with the following observations. The scribe uses both the forms *es* and *er*, the preposition *úr* is sometimes spelt *ýr*, *þ* is always written for both *ð* and *þ*, both *fyrir* and *yfir* are spelt with *i* rather than *y* and there is no overall consistency in distinguishing final *ð* and *t* in unstressed endings. *Ordbog* 1989, 458 dates the first part to c. 1220. If this is correct, the contents of the first part of the manuscript may have been translated in Iceland c. 1200, or even some time in the second half of the twelfth century. They would then be among the oldest sagas written in Iceland.

VI *Normalisation of the text*

A number of the orthographic features of the manuscript have been retained because they illustrate the scribal conventions of the time it was written and indicate the date of the manuscript, for example *ǫ́* has been used for *u*-mutation of *á* (later the two merged as *á*), and *þ* has been retained for *ð* throughout.

Abbreviations have been silently expanded. Abbreviations of Latin words such as *non*, *sed*, *dominus* used as abbreviations for common Icelandic words have been translated; other Latin words have been retained. Roman numerals have been translated into Icelandic.

Punctuation and paragraphing have been introduced to make the text easier to read. Capitals are used for proper names. The chapter divisions used by Unger in his edition have been followed.

Pointed brackets ⟨ ⟩ indicate that words or letters accidentally omitted by a copyist have been supplied by the editor. Square brackets [ ] are used for words that can no longer be read because of the state of the manuscript, but which can be reasonably assumed to have been written by the scribe. Where text was legible when Ludwig Larsson made his diplomatic transcript of AM 645 4to square brackets have not been used.

BIBLIOGRAPHY AND ABBREVIATIONS

Abdias, see Pseudo-Abdias.

The Ante-Nicene Fathers 8, 1995. Ed. Alexander Roberts and James Donaldson.

BHL = *Bibliotheca Hagiographica Latina* 1898–99 (reprinted 1992). Ed. Socii Bollandiani. *Novum Supplementum* 1986. Ed. Henricus Fros.

Cambridge History of Medieval English Literature 1999. Ed. D. Wallace.

Carron. H. C. [1994.] 'A Critical Edition of Pétrs saga Postola I, based on the Codex Scardensis'. Unpublished PhD thesis, University of London.

Clemoes, Peter, ed., 1997. *Ælfric's Catholic Homilies. The First Series. Text* (Early English Text Society SS. 17).

Cormack, Magaret, trans., 2000. 'Saga of Bishop Jón of Hólar'. In *Medieval Hagiography: an Anthology*. Ed. Thomas Head.

Cotelerius, J. B. 1672. *SS. Patrum qui temporibus Apostolicis floruerunt.* 2 vols.

Cullmann, Oscar 1962. *Peter, Disciple, Apostle, Martyr: A Historical and Theological Study.*

Fabricius, Johann Albert 1703–19. *Codex Apocryphus Novi Testamenti.*

Faulkes, Anthony 1983. 'Pagan Sympathy: Attitudes to Heathendom in the Prologue to *Snorra Edda*'. In *Edda: a Collection of Essays*. Ed. R. J. Glendinning and Haraldur Bessason, 283–314.

Foote, Peter 1994. 'Saints' Lives and sagas'. In *Saints and Sagas: a Symposium.* Ed. Hans Bekker-Nielsen, 73–88.

Funk, F. X. 1901. *Patres Apostolici* 2. Revised F. Diekamp 1913.

Gregory of Tours 1988. *Glory of the Martyrs.* Trans. Raymond van Dam (Translated texts for historians, Latin series III).

Hauksbók 1892–96. Ed. Finnur Jónsson and Eiríkur Jónsson.

Heilagra manna søgur 1877. Ed. C. R. Unger. 2 vols.

Hofmann, Dietrich 1997. *Die Legende von Sankt Clemens in den skandinavischen Ländern im Mittelalter.*

Holtsmark, Anne, ed., 1938. *A Book of Miracles. MS No. 645 4to of the Arna-Magnæan Collection in the University Library of Copenhagen* (Corpus Codicum Islandicorum Medii Aevi 12).

Honorius of Autun 1854. *Speculum Ecclesiæ.* In *PL* 172.

Hrafns saga Sveinbjarnarsonar 1987. Ed. Guðrún P. Helgadóttir.

Hreinn Benediktsson 1965. *Early Icelandic Script.*

ÍF = Íslenzkt fornrit I– , 1933– .

Jacobus de Voragine 1890. *Legenda Aurea.* Ed. Th. Graesse.

Jacobus de Voragine 1993. *The Golden Legend.* Trans. William Granger Ryan. 2 vols.

Johannes Diaconus Hymmonides and Bishop Gaudericus of Velletri 1968. *Vita sancti Clementis* I. In *Excerpta ex Clementinis Recognitionibus a Tyrannio Rufino translatis.* Ed. Ioannes Orlandi.

Jónas Kristjánsson 1981. 'Learned Style or Saga Style?'. In *Speculum Norroenum.* Ed. U. Dronke et al., 260–92.

Larsson, Ludwig, ed., 1885. *Isländska handskriften no 645 4to i den Arnamagnæanska Samlingen.*

Lipsius, R. A., ed., 1959. 'Passio sanctorum apostolorum Petri et Pauli'. In *Acta Apostolorum Apocrypha* I. Ed. R. A. Lipsius and M. Bonnet, 118–77.

Lönnroth, Lars 1969. 'The Noble Heathen: a Theme in the Sagas'. *Scandinavian Studies* 41, 1–29.

Mombritius, Boninus 1978. *Sanctuarium seu vitae sanctorum*. 2 vols.

New Catholic Encyclopedia 2003.

Nygaard, M. 1896. 'Den lærde stil i den norrøne prosa'. In *Sproglig-historiske Studier tilegnede Professor C. R. Unger*, 153–70.

ODCC = *The Oxford Dictionary of the Christian Church* 1983. Ed. F. L. Cross and E. A. Livingstone.

Ólafur Halldórsson, ed., 1994. *Mattheus saga postula* (Stofnun Árna Magnússonar á Íslandi, Rit 41).

Ordbog over det norrøne prosasprog. Registre 1989. Udgivet af den Arnamagnæanske Komission.

PG = Patrologia . . . Series Græca 1857–79. Ed. J. P. Migne.

PL = Patrologia . . . Series Latina 1844–64. Ed. J. P. Migne.

Plácidus saga 1998. Ed. John Tucker (Editiones Arnamagnæanæ B31).

Postola sögur 1874. Ed. C. R. Unger.

Pseudo-Abdias 1560. *De historia certaminis Apostolici*.

Pseudo-Marcellus, *Passio*. In Lipsius 1959.

Rehm, B., ed., 1965. *Die Pseudoklementinen* II. *Rekognitionen in Rufins Übersetzung*.

Stjórn 1862. Ed. C. R. Unger.

Sturlunga saga 1946. Ed. Jón Jóhannesson et al. 2 vols.

Trójumanna saga 1963. Ed. Jonna Louis-Jensen (Editiones Arnamangnæanæ A 8).

Turville-Petre, Gabriel 1953. *Origins of Icelandic Literature*.

Tveitane, Mattias 1985. 'Interpretatio norroena. Norrøne og antikke gudenavn i Clemens saga'. In *The Sixth International Saga Conference 28.7–2.8.1985. Workshop Papers* II, 1067–82.

Veraldar saga 1944. Ed. Jakob Benediktsson.

Vincent of Beauvais 1591. *Speculum Maius*.

Widding, O. et al., 1963. 'The Lives of the Saints in Old Norse Prose. A handlist'. *Mediaeval Studies* 25, 294–337.

CLEMENS SAGA

THE LIFE OF ST CLEMENT

I

Iulius hét inn fyrsti keiseri yfir ǫllum heimi ok af honum hafa allir
Rúmaborgarkonungar þat nafn tekit síþan. Iulius hét ǫþru namni Gaius.
3 Hann var fimm vetr einvaldi Rúmaborgarveldis. Hann vǫgu þeir Brutus
ok Cassius í Þórshofi í Rúmaborg ok margir aþrir ríkismenn meþ þeim
veittu áverk honum svát hann hafþi alls hálfan þriþia tøg sára á sér.
6 Systir Iulii hét Activa en hennar dóttir hét Octovia. Sonr Octov⟨i⟩e hét
Octov⟨i⟩anus es ǫþru namni var kallaþr Augustus. Hann hafþi veldi ifir
ǫllum heimi næstr eptir Iulium ok af honum er síþan Augustus kallaþr
9 hverr ifirkonungr Rúmaveldis. Augustus réþ firir Rúmaborgarríki sex
vetr ins sétta tegar. Hann setti friþ of allan heim ok á hans dǫgum var
Christus natus í þenna heim. Af þessum keiserum tveim hafa namn tekit
12 bókmánaþir tveir Julius ok Augustus.

Systrungar Augusti vǫru fratres þrír: Flavius es Clemens var kallaþr
ok gǫfgastr var allra Rúmveria undir Augusto keisera, en annarr
15 Faustinianus es frá mun verþa sagt, þriþi var Bassus es verstr var þeira
brœþra. Systir þeira brœþra var Plautilla es léþi Páli postola hǫfu⟨þ⟩dúks
síns þá er hann var leiddr til hǫggs. Hennar geldingar vǫru þeir Nereus
18 ok Achilleus es trú rétta tóku af kenningu Pétrs postola. Þá setti Plautilla
til at þióna dóttur sinni er hét [Fla]via Domitilla ok af þeira orþum varþ
Flavia kristin. En þeir vǫru báþir píndir firir Guþs sakar ok es messudagr
21 þeira viku eptir Crucis messu á várit.

II

Faustinianus hafþi veldi mikit undir Augustus keisera ok hann var settr
hǫfþingi ǫldunga í Rúmaborg ok hann hafþi forráþ heraþa es liggia í
24 nónd viþ Antiochia, Sýrlands hǫfuþborg. Kona hans hét Mathidia,
rúmversk at kyni. Hon var forkundliga væn at ifirliti ok ráþvǫnd harþla
ok vel viti borin, ok var iþin at blóta heiþin goþ. Maþr hennar var algerr
27 at sér at allri veraldarspekþ. Hann blótaþi skurgoþ at siþ Rúmveria, en
eigi af alhuga firir því at hann trúþi raunar einn vera almáttkan Guþ.

Þau Faustinianus ok Mathidia óttu þriá sonu. Einn hét Faustus, annarr
30 Faustinus, inn þriþi var heitinn eptir fǫþurbróþur sínum ok hét Clemens.

20 Flavio   24 Antiocho

THE LIFE OF ST CLEMENT

I

The first emperor over all the world was called Julius and all kings of Rome have since taken that name from him. Julius had Gaius as his other name. For five years he was sole ruler of the Roman Empire. Brutus and Cassius slew him in the Temple of Þórr in Rome and there were many other men of rank with them who inflicted wounds on him so that in all he had twenty-five wounds on his body. Julius's sister was called Activa and her daughter was called Octovia. Octovia's son was called Octovianus, who was called Augustus by his other name. He had authority over the whole world next after Julius and each supreme king of the Roman Empire has since been called Augustus after him. Augustus ruled over the Roman Empire for fifty-six years. He established peace throughout all the world and in his days Christ was born into this world. From these two emperors the two Latin months July and August have taken their names.

Three brothers were Augustus's cousins on his mother's side: Flavius, who was called Clement and was the noblest of all Romans under the Emperor Augustus, and the second was Faustinianus who will be told about later; the third was Bassus who was the worst of the brothers. The brothers' sister was Plautilla who lent the Apostle Paul her headscarf when he was taken to be beheaded. Nereus and Achilleus who received the true faith from the teaching of the Apostle Peter were her eunuchs. Plautilla appointed them to attend her daughter who was called Flavia Domitilla, and because of what they said Flavia became Christian. And they were both martyred for God's sake and their feastday is a week after Cross Mass in the spring.

II

Faustinianus held great authority under the Emperor Augustus and he was appointed leader of the senators in Rome and he had stewardship of districts which lie in the neighbourhood of Antioch, the capital city of Syria. His wife was called Mathidia, Roman by birth. She was extremely beautiful in appearance, and very upright and very intelligent, and was assiduous in worshipping heathen gods. Her husband was fully endowed with all worldly wisdom. He worshipped carven images in accordance with the Roman custom, but not wholeheartedly because he really believed in the existence of one almighty God.

Faustinianus and Mathidia had three sons. One was called Faustus, the second Faustinus, the third was named after his father's brother and called

En er þeir vǫru komnir ór barnœsku þá tók Bassus fǫþurbróþir þeira at
leggia girndarhug á Mathidiam móþur þeira ok bróþurkonu sína, ok
3 leitaþi hann til þess meþ fiǫlkyngi sinni ef hann mætti blekkia hana. En
er hon fann vilia hans óhœfan viþ sik, alls hon var ráþvǫnd kona, þá
leitaþi hon sér ráþs hvé hon mætti stýra bazt undan illsku hans. Hon bió
6 sik at þeim hætti sem hon var vǫn at búask þá er hon hafþisk at blótum
ok gekk síþan á málstefnu viþ búanda sinn ok mælti viþ hann:
   'Mér hefir lengi verit áhyggia at hvat leggiask muni firir sonu okkra.
9 Ek gekk of dag svá búin sem nú em ek í musteri sólargoþs es Apollo
heitir ok aldregi mun liúga. Ek fœrþa þar fórnir sólargoþi ok fréttak at
síþan hvat leggiask mundu firir sonu mína. En ek fekk þar þvílík svǫr:
12 "Takþu sonu þína tvá, Faustum ok Faustinum, ok bú þá til farar ok far
meþ þá til Sýrlands ok sel þá til fóstr⟨s⟩ inum fróþustum spekingum.
Þeir munu verþa gǫfgir kennimenn. En Clemens sonr þinn skal vera
15 heima meþ feþr sínum til huggunar honum ok mun at honum vegr vera
frændum hans ok ǫllum Rúmaborgar lýþ at eilífu."'
   Viþ þessi orþ varþ Faustinianus dapr harþla ok svaraþi af móþi miklum
18 ok mælti:
   'Ef þat er Guþs firirhyggia at svá skyli verþa sem þú segir, þá má engi
því hnekkia.'
21 Síþan bió hann skip gott ok gekk þar á kona hans ok synir hans tveir
inir ellri meþ fiárhlutum miklu⟨m⟩ ok fǫruneyti vegligu.

III

Þeim fórsk vel unz þeir liþu umb Sikiley. Þau fóru í nónd viþ borg þá es
24 Patera heitir ok Nicholaus byskup var síþan natus í. Þar tók þau
útsynningr steinóþr ok keyrþi of nótt at eyiu þeiri es Corpho heitir. Þar
leysti skip allt í sundr undir þeim ok fiárhlutir allir ok menn nema
27 Mathidia ok synir hennar. Þau ein hǫfþu líf. Hon fylgþi skipsborþi
nøkkveriu til lands ok gekk síþan á land upp. Hon kom of miþnætti til
húss einnar auþigs manns konu ok var þar tekit vel viþ henni. Þeir Faustus
30 ok Faustinus sǫtu á skipsflaki, ok es lýsa tók þá sǫ́ þeir fara í nónd sér
víkingaskip. Þeir le⟨i⟩tǫþu sér ráþs sín á milli hvat tiltœkiligast væri. Þá
mælti Faustus viþ Faustinum bróþur sinn:
33 'Þessir menn munu taka okkr ok selia mansali. Gefum vit okkr nǫmn
ǫnnur en vit eigum áþr. Ek mu⟨n⟩ nemnask Niceta, en þú skalt heita
Aquila.'

Clement. And when they were grown out of childhood, then Bassus, their father's brother, began to lust after Mathidia their mother and his brother's wife, and he attempted to see whether he could seduce her with his sorcery. And when she noticed his unseemly feelings towards her, since she was an upright woman, she tried to think of ways by which she might best escape his wickedness. She made herself ready in the way in which she usually prepared herself when she engaged in worship and then went to talk with her husband and said to him:

'For a long time I have been concerned about what our sons' future will be. I went during the day, dressed as I am now, into the temple of the Sun God who is called Apollo and will never lie. I brought offerings there to the Sun God and afterwards I asked what the future would be for my sons. And I received there these answers: "Take your two sons, Faustus and Faustinus, and prepare them for a journey and go with them to Syria and hand them over to be brought up by the wisest philosophers. They will become distinguished teachers. But your son Clement must remain at home with his father as a consolation to him and he will bring honour to his kinsmen and all the people of Rome for ever."'

At these words Faustinianus became very unhappy and answered in great sadness and said:

'If it is God's intention that it should be as you say, then no one can prevent it.'

Then he made ready a good ship, and his wife and his two elder sons boarded it with much treasure and a magnificent retinue.

III

Their voyage went well until they passed round Sicily. They sailed close to the city which is called Patera and in which Bishop Nicholas was later born. There a violent southwesterly gale caught them and swept them during the night to the island called Corfu. There the whole ship broke up beneath them and all goods and people except Mathidia and her sons. They alone survived. She came to land with the help of a ship's plank and then walked up ashore. She came at midnight to the house of a wealthy man's wife and she was received well there. Faustus and Faustinus sat on a piece of the wreckage, and when it began to grow light then they saw a pirate ship sailing near them. They discussed between themselves what would be most practical for them to do. Then Faustus said to his brother Faustinus:

'These men will seize us and sell us as slaves. Let us give ourselves other names than we already have. I shall call myself Niceta, and you shall be called Aquila.'

Síþan gripu víkingar sveina þessa báþa ok hǫfþu þá út of haf til Iórsalalands. Þeir seldu þá í siáborg þeiri es Cesarea heitir húsfreyiu
3 auþigri, ok hét sú Iusta ok var Gyþinga kyns. En húsfreyia sú lagþi ǫst mikla á sveinana ok gerþi þá sér at óskbǫrnum. Hon seldi þá til læringar Símoni inum fiǫ⟨l⟩kunga af Samaria es kraptr Guþs almáttigs lézk vera.
6 En er þeir hǫfþu numit allar íþróttir hans þá fundu þeir at hann loddi flærþ einni saman ok illsku. Þeir hliópusk á braut frá Símoni inum illa ok sóttu fund Pétrs postola. Hann tók viþ þeim vel ok kenndi þeim
9 kristinn dóm ok gerþusk þeir þá hans lærisveinar.

Mathidia hafþi virþingar góþar af húsfreyiu þeiri es viþ henni hafþi tekit. Hon var búin ítarliga fyrst þá er hon kom ór skipsbroti til húss
12 hennar, ok þóttisk húsfreyia þaþan af vita at hon myndi gǫfugmenni vera. Hon mælti of dag viþ hana:

'Þat þykiumk ek siá á þér at þú munt kynstór kona vera. Þú ert alvæn
15 ifirliz, látuþ vel ok vitrmál harþla, enda er hannǫrþ á hvívetna því es þú tekr þínum hǫndum til at gera. Nú vil ek at þú gerir mér húsbúnuþ ok búir klæþi es menn munu bera at hǫndum þér ok mun þér þat allt saman
18 verþa gott til fiár.'

Mathidia gerþi sem hon var beþin. Þaþan frá bǫru menn at henni klæþi mǫrg til gerþar. En hon gerþi svá at hverium var vel at skapi þeim es
21 átti. Þat varþ of unga menn es sǿ hana ok ásiónu hennar ok hannǫrþir á hverian veg vel gervar ok heyrþu orþalag hennar vitrligt at þeir lǫgþu á hana ástarhug mikinn. En hon veik undan at hafa þýþleik ne einn viþ
24 þá, en þeir kostgæfþu eigi at miþr at geta ǫst af henni. En þat varþ henni firir of dag at hon fór í fiǫru ok tók steina hvassa ok barþi þeim í andlit sér svát hon varþ ǫll blá ok blóþug of andlit. Síþan tók hon hinnu þunna
27 eþa roþ af fiski ok þanþi of andlit sér ok gerþi sik sem endimligsta á at siá. Hon meiddi ok hendr sínar meþ grióti at hon var til engrar sýslu fœr þeirar es vanda skyldi. Síþan fór hon til herbergis síns ok lézk vera
30 orþin firir vanheilsu. En þat harmaþi húsfreyia hennar fyrst ákafliga ok gerþi viþ hana vel ok miskunnsamliga of stundar sakar. En þaþan frá leiþ eigi langt unz hon lagþi á viþ hana órœkþ mikla ok gaf at henni
33 engi gaum.

Mathidia fann þat brátt at þá mátti ekki þar lengr vera viþ vanheilsu þá es hon hafþi. Þá fór hon braut ór þorpi því ok gekk til sævar. Þá sá
36 hon hús lítit þat riúka. Þat lauk hon upp ok hitti þar konu eina fátœkia es sat viþ glœþr ok kvaddi hon þá fyrri. Hon svaraþi ok mælti:

Afterwards the pirates seized both these boys and carried them off over the sea to Palestine. They then sold them in the sea town which is called Cesarea to a rich lady, and she was called Justa and was of Jewish family. And this lady came to love the boys greatly and made them her adoptive children. For their education she handed them over to Simon the Mage of Samaria who claimed to be the power of Almighty God. And when they had learnt all his skills then they realised that he held fast to nothing but deceit and wickedness. They ran away from Simon the Evil and went to see the Apostle Peter. He welcomed them and taught them Christianity and they then became his disciples.

Mathidia was treated decently by the housewife who had taken her in. She was finely dressed at first when she came to her house from the shipwreck, and the housewife thought that she could tell from this that she must be a person of rank. She spoke to her one day:

'I think that I can see from looking at you that you must be a high-born woman. You have a very fair appearance, are well-mannered and are extremely wise in speech, moreover there is skill in whatever you set your hands to do. Now I should like you to make me hangings for the house and make up cloth that people will bring to you and altogether this will make a good source of income for you.'

Mathidia did as she was asked. From then on people brought many clothes to her for sewing. And she sewed them so that everyone was very pleased who owned them. It happened with young men who saw her and her appearance and her fine work in every way well made, and heard her sensible way of speaking, that they fell deeply in love with her. And she avoided having any familiarity with them, but they strove none the less to win love from her. And she ended up going to the beach one day and picking up sharp stones and beating them on her face so that she was all blue and bloody in her face. Then she took a thin membrane or skin of a fish and stretched it across her face and made herself as outlandish as possible to look at. She also injured her hands with stones so that she was incapable of doing anything that required intricate work. Then she went to her room and said that she had fallen ill. And her housewife was extremely upset about her at first and treated her well and kindly for a while. But from then on it was not long before she began to neglect her badly and paid no heed to her.

Mathidia soon realised that she could no longer remain there in her poor state of health. Then she left that village and walked to the sea. Then she saw smoke rising a little from a house. She opened it and found a poor woman there who was sitting by the embers, and she greeted her first. She answered and said:

'Vel þú komin, dróttning mín. Allt mitt skal þitt vera. Ertu húsfreyia
en rúmverska, sú er komt ein á land þá er allt fǫruneyti þitt fórsk? Mikill
3 harmr es þat er þú ert svá aum orþin. Vestu meþ mér svá lengi sem þú
vill ok skaldu ein ǫllu ráþa því es ek á.'
      Þeim orþum varþ Mathidia svá fegin at hon felldi tǫr. Síþan mælti
6 hon viþ þá es firir bió:
      'Fir hví es þú komin í kot þetta?'
      Hon svaraþi: 'Firir nøkkverium vetrum missta ek búanda míns svát vit
9 óttum engi erfingia, en ek vilda ein vera firir mér eptir dag hans. Fór ek af
því á braut ór borg ok bǫrluþumk hér firir. Nú á ek akr nekkvern ok fá þá
sauþi til atvinnu mér. Ek hefi nú fengit líkþrǫ ok má ek nú ekki at hafask.'
12 Þá mælti Mathidia: 'Ek mun vera hér ok hugga þik ok þióna þér unz
enn koma betri dagar ifir okkr.'
      En frá þeim degi fór Mathidia of þorp ok borgir ok baþ firir þær matar
15 ok burgusk þær þá viþ þat. Í þeim staþ hǫfþusk þær viþ lítils vant tuttugu
vetr unz þær fingu miskunn af fundi ins helga Pétrs postola sem síþarr
mun frá verþa sagt nakkvat.

IV

18 Nú skal þar til máls at taka es Faustinianus, faþir þeira brœþra Faustus
ok Faustinus, þá er hann spurþi tíþindi þessi at skip þat hafþi farizk viþ
Corpho es kona hans var á ok sønir, hann hugþi at þau mundu ǫll þar
21 tapazk hafa. Hann kunni því svá illa at hann lagþisk í rekkiu af ok þótti
nær sem hann væri af viti ginginn í harmi sínum. Þá fór Bassus bróþir
hans til fundar viþ hann ok lét megingóþvættliga, en illt bió undir. Hann
24 kvaddi bróþur sinn blíþliga ok mælti:
      'Sé ek bróþir at þú ert dapr harþla af mannamissi þeim es þú hyggsk
fenginn hafa. En hitt er ráþ at huggask ok gerask staþramr viþ þótt þér
27 þyki eigi allt at vilia þínum siálfs ganga. Kona þín hefir komit á land
meþ miklu⟨m⟩ fiárhlutum ok es nú í austrhólfu heims langt á braut ýr
Rúmveriaveldi. Hon es nú gefin einum þræli sínum þeim es lengi hefir
30 virkþamaþr hennar verit.'
      Viþ þessi tíþendi varþ Faustinianus styggr miǫk ok mátti lengi eigi
orþi upp koma. Hann settisk upp ok mælti:
33 'Hvat ætlar þú, bróþir, hver stiarna því mun valda meþ skǫpum er svá
illa hefir snúizk skap konu minnar?'

15 vart

'Welcome, my mistress. Everything of mine shall be yours. Are you the Roman lady who came ashore alone when all your companions perished? It is a great sorrow that you have become so wretched. Stay with me as long as you wish, and you alone shall manage all that I have.'

At these words Mathidia was so happy that she shed tears. Then she said to the woman who dwelt there:

'Why have you come to this cottage?'

She answered: 'Some winters ago I lost my husband without our having any heirs, and I wanted to be on my own after his time. So I left the city and struggled to get along here. Now I own a field and these few sheep for my livelihood. I have now caught leprosy and I am now unable to do anything.'

Then Mathidia said: 'I will stay here and comfort you and look after you until better days come for us again.'

And from that day Mathidia went throughout villages and towns and begged for food for them and they managed to survive on that. They lived in that place a little short of twenty years until they had the good fortune to meet the Blessed Apostle Peter about which something will be told later.

IV

Now we shall take up the story again at the point where Faustinianus, the father of the brothers Faustus and Faustinus, when he heard this news that the ship had been lost off Corfu which his wife and sons were aboard, he thought that they must all have perished there. He felt so distressed by this that he took to his bed and it seemed almost as if he had lost his reason in his sorrow. Then his brother Bassus went to see him and spoke very kindly, but there was evil behind it. He greeted his brother cheerfully and said:

'I see, brother, that you are extremely sad on account of the bereavements which you believe you have suffered. But it is more sensible to be comforted and make yourself steadfast though it seems to you everything does not go according to your own wishes. Your wife has come ashore with much treasure and is now in the eastern part of the world far away from the Roman Empire. She is now wedded to one of her slaves who has been her favourite for a long time.'

At this news Faustinianus became very upset and for a long time was not able to utter a word. He sat up and said:

'What do you think, brother, which star by destiny can be the cause that my wife's disposition has changed so much for the worse?'

Bassus mælti: 'Gǫngum vit í virkþahús þat es vit eigum ok allr stiǫrnugangr es markaþr í.'

3   En er þeir vǫru þangat komnir þá mælti Bassus: 'Sér þú nú hér bróþir hversu stiǫrnurnar ganga?'

Hann svaraþi: 'Víst sé ek.'

6   Bassus mælti: 'Þikistu skilia mega hvar Friggiar stiarna mun staþit hafa á getnaþartíþ eþa burþartíþ konu þinnar?'

Faustinianus mælti: 'Ekki má ek ætlun á slíkt koma firir harmi þeim
9   es ek hefik beþit.'

Þá mælti Bassus: 'Þat þykiumk ek vita at á burþartíþ konu þinnar mun Friggiar stiarna staþit hafa í þeim staþ sem sól kømr upp þá er dagr
12 es skemstr. En sú kona es svá verþr borin má at ǫngum kosti ráþvǫnd vera ef hon verþr fulltíþa.'

Viþ þessi orþ varþ Faustinianus ókvæþi meþ ǫllu ok viþ þat es hann
15 dixit slíkt ok vildi hann ekki lengr rœþa viþ bróþur sinn. Hann tók at heita á inn eina Guþ at hann skyldi því skióta í hug honum es honum gegndi helzt hvat hann legþi firir sik þaþan frá. Þá minntisk hann á þat
18 at hann hafþi veldi ifir heruþum þeim es liggia viþ Anþekiu. Honum þótti ok þaþra glíkligast til at hann mǫndi nakkvat mega spyria til konu sinnar eþa sona. Síþan bió hann skip mikit ok skrautligt harþla ok gekk
21 þar á skip ipse meþ fǫruneyti miklu. Hann helt skipi því í Grikklandshaf ok horfþisk fyrst miǫk vænliga á á farlengþ hans, en hinn veg lauk þó at of nótt keyrþi skip þat í óþaveþri at biǫrgum nøkkverium í ey þeiri es
24 Ciprus heitir ok Norþmenn kalla Kípr. Þá brotnaþi skip þat allt í sundr ok týndusk fiárhlutir allir þeir es á skipinu vǫru ok engi maþr komsk á land nema Faustinianus einn ok varþ honum viþ bana siálfan. En er
27 hann tók hvíld á landi ok lýsa tók þá kenndi hann hvar hann var kominn. Hann gekk í borg nøkkvera litla ok fekk hann þar góþar viþtǫkur, en engi maþr kenndi hann þar. Hann gekk þar í sýslu mikla ok gerþisk
30 hann þar varþmaþr í borg þeiri. Þá sýslu hafþi hann átián vetr eþa litlu miþr unz þingat kom Petrus postoli ok kenndi honum trú rétta.

V

Á ári inu þriþia eptir píning Dróttins ok á inu tíunda ári veldis Tiberii
33 keisera þá kom Barnabas postoli af Iórsalalandi á skipi til Rúmaborgar ok fór of nótt í stiga upp í borgina. Ok tók hann þegar inn sama dag at bióþa trú rétta ok sanna es hann kom í borgina. En menn lǫgþu eigi

Bassus said: 'Let us go into the special room which we have and in which the whole course of the stars is marked.'

And when they had come there, then Bassus said: 'Do you see here now, brother, how the stars go?'

He answered: 'Indeed I see.'

Bassus said: 'Do you think you can work out where the star of Frigg will have been at the time of your wife's conception or birth?'

Faustinianus said: 'I cannot calculate such a thing because of the sorrow I have suffered.'

Then Bassus said: 'I feel certain that at the time of your wife's birth the star of Frigg must have been in the position where the sun rises when day is shortest. And the woman who is born thus can by no means be upright if she becomes adult.'

At these words Faustinianus became utterly speechless and because he said these things, then he would not talk further with his brother. He began to pray to the one God that he might put into his mind the best course for him to follow from then on. Then he remembered that he had authority over those regions which lie near Antioch. He also thought it most likely that he would be able to hear some news of his wife or his sons there. Then he prepared a large and very splendid ship and boarded the ship himself with a large company. He sailed the ship into the Ægean Sea and at first his voyage promised very well, but it ended otherwise, however, that the ship was driven during the night in a violent gale onto certain cliffs on the island which is called Ciprus and which the Northmen call Kípr. Then the ship broke up completely and all the goods that were on the ship were lost and no one got ashore except only Faustinianus, and he was close to death itself. And when he had had a rest on the shore and dawn broke he recognised where he had come. He walked to a certain small town and was made welcome there, but no one there knew him. He took on important work there and he became watchman in the town. He held that position for eighteen years or a little less until the Apostle Peter came there and taught him the true faith.

V

In the third year after the Passion of Christ and in the tenth year of the reign of the Emperor Tiberius, the Apostle Barnabas came by ship from Palestine to Rome and in the night climbed up a ladder into the city. And on the same day he got into the city he at once began to preach the right and true faith. But the men who listened did not have a high opinion of his

miklar virþingar á tǫlur hans þeir es til hlýddu. Þar kom fram maþr ungr
ok búinn ítarliga meþ ríþerasveit mikla ok kvaddi sér hlióþs.	En hann

3	hóf svá mál sitt:

'Hví verþr yþr þat firir Rúmverium at gera í gegn borgarsiþ ok lǫgum
órum ok taka eigi betr viþ ørendreka Guþs, þeim es boþar hiǫlp ok

6	heilsu ǫllum heimi at því er ek hygg?'

Þá gafsk hlióþ gott af alþýþu. Síþan laut sá inn ungi maþr Barnabe
postola ok kvaddi hann á þessa lund:

9	'Heilldu ok vel kominn sanctus postoli Guþs Domini nostri Jesu
Christi! Segþu oss frá hingatkomu Christi í þenna heim ok frá burþ
hans ok tóknum þeim es hann gerþi ok frá kenningum, frá píningu hans

12	ok upprisu af dauþa, frá uppsti⟨g⟩ning til himna ok frá tilkomu Sancti
Spiritus es hann gaf postolum sínum. Ok svá vilium vér at þú segir oss
frá annarri hingatkomu hans, þá er hann skal koma í enda veraldar at

15	dœma of allt mannkyn ok láta hvern hafa þat es til gørir meþ Guþs
miskunn.'

Þá tók Barnabas postoli at greiþa þat mál allt sem hann var beiddr, ok

18	hlýddi þá ǫll alþýþa vel unz hann lauk kenningu sinni sem hann vildi.
Síþan tók sá inn ungi maþr viþ honum í herbergi sínu ok fekk honum
alla reiþu gnógliga ok boþaþi þingat þeim mǫnnum ǫllum es heyra vildu

21	orþ Guþs.

Fǫm dǫgum síþarr mælti sá inn ungi húsbúandi viþ Barnaban postola:
'Ek vil segia þér deili á mér ok á kyni mínu. Ek heiti Clemens en faþir

24	minn Faustinianus, systrungr Augustus keisera. Ek varþveiti at forráþi
fǫþur míns alla fǫþurleifþ mína ok emk nú hálfþrítøgr maþr at aldri. Nú
vilia menn, sem þú sér ipse, eigi miǫk skipask viþ kenningar þínar ok

27	má vera at sé af því at þér sé heldr annarstaþar ávǫxtr at taka af
kenningum þínum. Nú farþu í nafni Domini til Sýrlands ok er þú fiþr
inn helga Pétr hǫfþingia postola þá berþu honum kveþiu mína rœkiliga

30	ok seg svá at á ǫþru ári mun ek koma til hans ef ek lifi, ok mun ek biþia
at hann komi hingat í borg þessa. Þat þyki mér áræþiligt at Guþ mun
hafa ætlat at senda sinn inn hæsta postola ok ørendreka í ina œztu

33	hǫfuþborg heimsins at snúa þeim lýþ til Guþs es þessa borg byggvir.'

Eptir þat lét Clemens búa farskost góþan til handa Barnabe postola
ok fekk alla reiþu á skip þat þá er hann þurfti at hafa. Síþan leiddi

36	Clemens Barnaban til skips ok baþ honum vel farask ok fal sik meþ
tǫrum undir bœnir hans es þeir skilþusk. En skip þat er Barnabas postoli

speeches. A man came forward there, young and finely dressed, with a large company of mounted men, and called for a hearing. And he began his speech so:

'Why does it come about for you Romans that you go against civility and our laws and do not receive God's messenger better, who proclaims salvation and healing to all the world according to my view?'

Then there was complete silence from all the people. Afterwards the young man bowed down to the Apostle Barnabas and greeted him in this way:

'Greetings and welcome, holy Apostle of our Lord God Jesus Christ! Tell us about the coming of Christ into this world and about his birth and the miracles which he did and about his teachings, about his Passion and Resurrection from death, about his Ascension into heaven and about the coming of the Holy Ghost which he gave to his Apostles. And we also wish you to tell us about his second coming, when he shall come at the end of the world to judge all mankind and let each man have what he deserves by God's grace.'

Then the Apostle Barnabas began to expound everything that he was asked, and then all the people listened attentively until he finished his preaching as he wished. Then the young man received him into his lodging and provided him plentifully with everything he needed and invited everyone there who wished to hear the word of God.

A few days later the young master of the house spoke to the Apostle Barnabas:

'I will tell you about myself and my family. I am called Clement, and my father Faustinianus, a cousin of the Emperor Augustus. I am looking after all my patrimony by my father's authority and I am now twenty-five years old. Now people are unwilling, as you yourself see, to change their ways much at your teaching and it may be that it is because the fruit of your teaching is to be gathered elsewhere. Now go to Syria in the Lord's name and when you find the Blessed Peter, leader of the Apostles, then give him my sincere greetings and say that next year I will come to him if I live, and I shall ask him to come here to this city. It seems likely to me that God will have intended to send his chief Apostle and messenger into the most important capital city of the world to turn the people to God who live in this city.'

After that Clement had a good vessel made ready for the Apostle Barnabas and provided all the equipment on the ship which he needed to have. Then Clement took Barnabas to the ship and bade him fare well and with tears commended himself to his prayers when they parted. And the ship that the Apostle Barnabas was on went with good speed until it halted

var á fór greitt unz þat nam staþar firir útan haf í borg þeiri es Cesarea
heitir. Þar var Petrus postoli firir ok í húsum þess manns es Zacheus
3   heitir ok þá hafþi byskupdóm tekit ifir þeiri borg af Petro postola. Sá
inn sami Zacheus es nefndr in evangelio til þess at hann gerþi fǫgnuþ
Domino nostro í húsum sínum í borg þeiri es Iericho heitir.

6   En á ǫþru ári kom til þeirar borgar innar sǫmu af Rúmaborg Clemens,
frændi Augusti k⟨e⟩isera ok sonr Faustinianus ok Mathidie. Viþ honum
tóku allir borgarmenn vel ok allra bazt þeir es kristnir vǫru. Þá minntisk
9   Barnabas postoli á þat hversu vel Clemens hafþi hans mǫlum tekit í
Rúmaborg. Hann fylgþi honum á fund Pétrs postola, en hann tók viþ
honum feginsamliga vel. En fǫm dǫgum síþarr var þing fiǫlmennt á
12   stræti nær húsum þeim es Zacheus byskup átti. Í borginni var stǫpull
hǫr miǫk. Þar hafþi herbergi í stǫpli þeim Símon inn illi ok inn fiǫlkungi
ok vera lézk kraptr Guþs. Hann talþisk vera sólin ipsa, en konu sína
15   kallaþi hann tungl vera es kvenkenndu namni heitir luna á latínu tungu.
Stiǫrnur þær fimm es lausar fara í lopti ok planete heita at bókmáli,
talþi hann þær ambáttir vera konu sinnar. Símon inn illi hafþi fyrst skírn
18   tekit af Philippo es einn var af diáknum siau inum fyrstum. Síþan var
hann bannsettr af postolum Domini Petro ok Iohanne firir þat at hann
hugþisk at fékaupum myndu gera Helgan Anda. Vildi hann hans giptir
21   fé kaupa ok viþ fé selia í gegn því es Dominus mælti viþ postola sína of
Helgan Anda:
      'At vingiǫf ok ǫst heilagri þǫguþ ér Helgan Anda enda skuluþ ér
24   félaust veita.'
      En á nemndum degi kom Petrus postoli Guþs til þings ok gekk at
þingstǫþinni neþan frá sió. Þingat kom ok Clemens meþ mikla sveit, þá
27   er undir Rúmveria vǫru hallir. Þar kom ok Símon inn illi meþ sveit sína
ok sat hann á ofanverþu stræti í nónd viþ stǫpul sinn. Á þingi því reis
upp Pétr postoli fyrstr allra manna ok kvaddi allan lýþ á þessa lund:
30   'Friþr sé yþr ǫllum es af ǫllu hiarta ok af ǫllum krapti elskiþ Dominum
Guþ yþvarn.'
      Þá svaraþi Símon magus: 'Eigi þurfum vér friþ af þér at þiggia.'
33   Þá mælti Petrus: 'Fir hví máttu eigi heyra friþ boþaþan? Af synþum
ok af lǫstum hlýzk iamnan sundrþyki ok bardagi en friþi fylgia allir
kostir ok ǫll fríþendi.'

7 Augusto   23 vinbgjǫf

the other side of the sea in the city which is called Caesarea. The Apostle Peter was there and in the dwelling of a man called Zacheus who had then taken over the bishopric of the city from the Apostle Peter. This same Zacheus is mentioned in the Gospel because he made our Lord welcome in his dwelling in the city which is called Jericho.

And the next year Clement, kinsman of the Emperor Augustus and son of Faustinianus and Mathidia, came to the same city from Rome. All the citizens received him well and best of all those who were Christians. Then the Apostle Barnabas called to mind how well Clement had received his sermons in Rome. He took him to see the Apostle Peter, and he welcomed him joyfully. And a few days later there was a crowded assembly in the street close to the house which Bishop Zacheus had. There was a very high tower in the city. Simon the Evil and the Mage had a room there in the tower and claimed that he was the power of God. He reckoned that he was the sun itself, and he maintained that his wife was the moon which is called *luna*, a feminine word in the Latin language. The five stars which move freely in the sky and which are called planets in Latin, he claimed that they were his wife's handmaidens. Simon the Evil had first received baptism from Philip, who was one of the first seven deacons. Afterwards he was excommunicated by the Lord's Apostles Peter and John because he thought that he was going to make a profit out of the Holy Ghost. He wanted to buy its gifts with money and to sell them for money, contrary to what the Lord said to his Apostles concerning the Holy Ghost:

'You received the Holy Ghost as a gift of friendship and holy love and moreover you shall bestow it without payment (cf. Acts 8:14–24).'

And on the appointed day God's Apostle Peter came to the assembly and walked to the assembly-place from down by the sea. Clement also came there with a large company of men, those who favoured the Romans. Simon the Evil also came there with his group and he sat in the upper part of the street near his tower. At this assembly the Apostle Peter got up before anyone else and greeted all the people in this way:

'Peace be with you all who with all your heart and with all your might love your Lord God.'

Then Simon Magus answered: 'We do not need to receive peace from you.'

Then Peter said: 'Why can you not hear peace proclaimed? Discord and battle are always the result of sins and vices but all virtues and benefits come with peace.'

Þá mælti Símon: 'Hitt es nú ráþ at þú ger ónýtt mál mitt ef þú mátt
nøkkveria flærþ finna í orþum mínum.

3   Ek mun ok kosta at ónýta
kenningar þínar es lokleysu einni loþa saman, ok mun ek sýna hvat it
sanna er ⟨at⟩ til þurftar ok til hiálpar sé allri alþýþu.'
     Þá mælti Petrus: 'Fœrum vit fram ok þá mǫl okkur meþ hófsemi ok

6   skapgœþi.'
     Símon svaraþi: 'Enskis eru verþ mǫl þín ǫll.'
     Þá kallaþi sá inn illi karl Símon hótt meþ ǫllu ok mælti:

9   'Hlýþiþ mér allir menn þeir es hér eruþ komnir. Ek emk kraptr
almáttigs skapera. Ek komk af himnum ofan ok vask getinn í kviþi konu
þeiri es Rakel hét. Hon fœddi mik tíu vetr vandliga. En einn hvern dag

12   seldi hon í hǫnd mér sigþ ok sendi hon mik til kornskurþar. Ek kom til
akrsins ok mælta ek viþ sigþinn: "Skerþu nú kornit." Hann skar akrinn
eigi seinna en tíu menn. Mér es hlýþin ǫll skepna til þess es ek vil. Ek

15   má fliúga í lopti í eldslíki. Ek geri svá at aldintré eþa akr rennr þar upp
sem ek vil. Ek má fara í gegnum fiǫll hvars ek vil. At boþorþi mínu
hlæia líkneski þau es ger eru ór tré eþa ór málmi ok hrœrask þau ok

18   mæla ef ek býþ þat. Ek skipti ifirlitum mínum ef ek vil svát ek sýnumk
stundum gamall maþr ok skeggiaþr miǫk ok hárr, en stundum fulltíþi
maþr ok nakkvat skeggiaþr, en stundum sýnumk ek gransprettingr eþa

21   yngri ok svá ungr ok stundum ungmenni. Stundum bregþ ek á mik
kykvenda líki ýmissa, fogla eþa orma, fiska eþa dýra, nauta eþa hrossa,
hrúta eþa hafra.'

24   Þá er Símon talþi slíkt firir lýþnum þá andsvaraþi Petrus postoli:
'Sýnisk yþr eigi sem siá siálfr diǫfulsmaþr lýsi ifir fiǫlkyngi sinni ok
flærþ í sínum orþum, en eigi of go⟨þ⟩dómi þeim es hann lézk hafa ok

27   hann hefir þó at øngum kosti?'
     Lýþrinn svaraþi: 'At vísu sýnisk oss svá.'
     Þá mælti Petrus viþ Símon: 'Hvílíkir munu þeir menn verþa es hverfa

30   eptir þér?'
     Símon svaraþi: 'Svá sem ek em siálfr eilífr ok ódauþligr, svá munu
ok allir mínir menn aldregi deyia.'

33   Petrus mælti: 'Hvárt trúir þú upprisu dauþra manna?'
     Símon svaraþi: 'Eigi, eigi.'
     Petrus mælti: 'Hví vildu liúga? Þat veit ek at þú hefir í vitum þínum

36   lík barns þess es þú ipse banaþir ok gengr þú viþ þat til fréttar. En ór
þeim inum litla búk veitir diǫfull þér andsvǫr of þá hluti es þú spyrr at.

Then Simon said: 'What you must do now is demonstrate the wrongness of my position if you can find any falsehood in my words. I shall also try to refute your teachings which consist of pure nonsense, and I shall show what the truth is which is to the profit and salvation of all people.'

Then Peter said: 'Let us then also present our cases with moderation and good nature.'

Simon answered 'All your words are worthless.'

Then this evil fellow Simon absolutely shouted out loud and said:

'All those men who have come here listen to me! I am the power of the Almighty Creator. I came down from heaven and I was conceived in the womb of a woman who was called Rakel. She reared me carefully for ten years. And one day she put a sickle in my hand and she sent me to reap corn. I came to the field and said to the sickle: "Now cut the corn!" It cut the field no slower than ten men. Every creature is obedient to me for whatever I wish. I can fly in the air in the form of fire. I make it so that fruit-trees or crops grow up where I wish. I can go through mountains wherever I wish. At my bidding those images laugh which are made of wood or metal and if I command it they move and speak. I change my appearance if I so wish so that sometimes I appear as an old man and very bearded and hoary, and sometimes as a full grown man and slightly bearded, and sometimes I appear as an adolescent or younger, and as young also sometimes as a child. Sometimes I put on the forms of various living creatures, birds or snakes, fish or wild animals, cattle or horses, rams or goats.'

When Simon had spoken these things before the people then the Apostle Peter answered:

'Does it not appear to you that this servant of the Devil is himself proclaiming his sorcery and deceit by his words, and not that divinity which he claimed to have and which he in no way has?'

The people answered: 'Certainly it seems so to us.'

Then Peter said to Simon: 'What will those men become who follow you?'

Simon answered: 'Just as I myself am eternal and immortal, so also all my men will never die.'

Peter said: 'Do you believe in the resurrection of the dead?'

Simon answered: 'No, no.'

Peter said: 'Why will you lie? I know this, that in your inner chamber you have the corpse of a child which you yourself killed and you go to it to ask about the future. And from that small body the devil gives you answers concerning the matters which you ask about. Let us now go who believe

Fǫrum vér nú es á Christum trúum ok rannsǫkum vit Símonar ok vitum
hvat vér finnum þar.'

3   Þá er Petrus mælti þessi orþ þá sýndisk mǫnnum sicut Símon flygi
í lopt upp, enda hvarf hann allr hiá stǫpli sínum. Þá var ok komit at
nótt ok tók þá at myrkva miǫk es Símon hvarf. Þá mælti Petrus viþ allan lýþ:
6   'Nú megu þér siá at Símon vill eigi láta rannsaka vit sín. Fariþ ér nú í
Guþs friþi hverr í hús sitt ok komiþ til mín at morni árdegis. Þá skuluþ
ér heyra formæli mitt ok þá mun lýsask firir yþr saþr Guþs kraptr til
9   hiálpar ǫndum yþrum ok líkǫmum ok heþan af mun eyþask átrúnuþr
viþ Símon af því at menn megu allir vita meþ hvé mikil svik hann ferr.'

Annan dag eptir kom fiǫlþi manna á fund Pétrs postola árdegis. En
12 þá var Símon horfinn ór borginni meþ allt sitt ok lengi síþan vissu menn
ekki til hans í þeim heruþum. Þann dag talþi Petrus lengi firir lýþnum
ok gerþi kunna allri alþýþu flærþ Símonar. Þá gaf hann ok heilsu mǫrgum
15 siúkum mǫnnum, þeir es þar kómu til hans. Þaþan kristnaþisk fiǫlþi
manna ok tók skírn í namni Domini. Ok þá var Clemens þar skírþr ok
allt fǫruneyti hans, ok rézk hann til fylgiu viþ Pétr postola ⟨ok baþ hann
18 Pétr postola⟩ at hann skyldi fara til Rúmaborgar at boþa þar Guþs ørendi
þeim mǫnnum es þar vildi heyra. En hann lézk fyrst mundu reka Guþs
ørendi á Gyþingalandi sicut honum var boþit af Guþi, en loks lét hann
21 vón at hann mundi vitia Rúmaborgar á firirætlaþ⟨r⟩i tíþ af Guþi ok
kallaþisk hann þar mǫndu enda líf sitt at Guþs vilia.

Síþan boþaþi Pétr postoli Guþs namn of Gyþingaland allt ok of Sýrland
24 ok of Grikklandseyiar ok þau heruþ es þar eru í nónd. En Clemens fylgþi
honum hvar sem hann fór. Þeir Niceta ok Aquila, brœþr Clementis,
vóru þá iamnan í fylgiu meþ Petro, ok kǫnnuþusk þeir þó ekki viþ
27 Clementem í þann tíþ at þeir væri brœþr hans.

Svá bar at at skip þat es Petrus postoli var á kom viþ ey þá es Corpho
heitir. Þá er þeir dvǫldusk þar í einni hverri hǫfn, þá gengu þeir Niceta
30 ok Aquila of dag á land upp. Þeir kómu þar es leikstefna nøkkver var
fiǫlmenn ok tóku þeir at boþa þeim mǫnnum á fund Pétrs postola es
heyra vildu Guþs orþ eþa kenning helga eþa fá bót meina sinna, þeir es
33 þar væri vanheilir. Þar kom Mathidia at gangandi ok nemndisk ǫþru
na⟨m⟩ni en hon átti. Hon mælti viþ þá Nicetam ok Aquilam:

---

14 kunna] + flærð   17–18 *words supplied by* Unger   26 kǫnnuðisk

in Christ and search Simon's inner chamber and see what we find there.'

When Peter had spoken these words then it seemed to people as if Simon flew up in the air, indeed he completely disappeared near his tower. Then also night had fallen and it began to grow very dark when Simon disappeared. Then Peter said to all the people:

'Now you can see that Simon does not want to have his inner chamber searched. Go now in God's peace each to his house and come to me early in the morning. Then you shall hear my preaching and then the true power of God will be revealed to you for the salvation of your souls and bodies and from now on belief in Simon will be destroyed because everyone will be able to see with what great deceit he behaves.'

The next day a multitude of people came early in the morning to see the Apostle Peter. But then Simon had disappeared from the town with all his belongings and for a long time afterwards men knew nothing of him in those regions. That day Peter preached for a long time before the people and he made Simon's deceit known to all the population. Then he also gave health to many sick people who came to him there. From then on many people became Christians and received baptism in the name of the Lord. And then Clement was baptised and all his companions and he became a follower of the Apostle Peter and he asked the Apostle Peter to go to Rome to preach God's message to those people who were willing to hear him there. But he said that he would first carry out God's mission in the land of the Jews as he was commanded by God, but he said he expected that he would in the end visit Rome at a time preordained by God and declared that there he would end his life in accordance with God's will.

Afterwards the Apostle Peter preached God's name throughout all the land of the Jews and throughout Syria and the Greek Islands and those districts which were round about. And Clement went with him wherever he went. Clement's brothers, Niceta and Aquila, were then always in Peter's company, and yet at that time they did not realise who Clement was, that they were his brothers.

It happened that the ship which the Apostle Peter was on called at the island which is called Corfu. While they were staying there in a certain harbour, then one day Niceta and Aquila went up ashore. They came to where there was a certain crowded games meeting and they began to call on those people to come to see the Apostle Peter who wanted to hear God's word or holy teaching or to receive a cure for their ailments, those there who were ill. Mathidia came walking up and called herself by another name than her own. She spoke to Niceta and Aquila:

'Hvers vætti þit, hvárt mér mon at nøkkverri hiálp verþa ef ek kømk á fund Pétrs postola?'

3 Þeir svǫruþu: 'Ef þú ert saþr þurfamaþr, enda vildu trúa á Iesum Christum, son Guþs, þá mundu víst miskunn fá af fundi hans sem allir þeir es at flærþlausu vilia hans kenningar heyra ok hafa.'

6 Annars dags kom Mathidia af tilvísun þeira á fund Pétrs postola ok fell til fóta honum ok baþ hann ǫlmusugiafar. Petrus mælti: 'Af hví þarftu at þiggia ǫlmusugiafar eigi óheillig kona nú at því es
9 mér sýnisk?'

Hon svaraþi: 'Freyva mín es vanheil ok líkþrǫ́, ok vinn ek til reiþu okkr báþum. Af því biþ ek þik ǫlmusugiafa.'

12 Petrus mælti: 'Hvat skyldir þik til at vinna firir konu þeiri?'

Þá er Mathidia skyldi þat segia, þá komsk hon viþ ákafliga miǫk ok mátti øngu orþi upp koma. Þá mælti Petrus postoli:

15 'Þat er ætlun mín at þú munt verit hafa kona gǫfug at metorþum ok auþig, en nú kømr þér í hug ævi þín in fyrri ok skammask þú nú válaþs þíns ok vesalþar er nú es ifir þik komin.'

18 Mathidia mælti: 'Rétt ætlar þú nú, herri minn,' kvaþ hon Mathidia viþ postolann.

Petrus mælti: 'Komi hingat húsfreyia þín, ok siǫm vér hvat síþan
21 gerisk af.'

Þá var sýst til þess at húsfreyiu hennar var fylgt þingat til fundar viþ Pétr postola, ok var hon lǫgþ firir fœtr postolans. Þá mælti hann viþ
24 þær báþar:

'Viliþ it trúa á Guþ fǫþur almáttkan ok á son hans Iesum Christum Dominum nostrum ok á Helgan Anda?'

27 Þær svǫruþu: 'Víst monum vit trúa sem þú kennir.'

Síþan signdi Petrus ina siúku konu ok varþ hon þegar heil af líkþrǫ́ sinni. En því næst vǫ́ru þær skírþar báþar í namni Þrenningar. Þá fór sú
30 kona es heilsuna hafþi fengit til frændliþs síns meþ leyfi Pétrs postola. Mathidia tók at biþia at hon skyldi ná at fylgia Petro postola ok girndisk hon at heyra kenningar hans of daga, enda var henni þat veitt. Hon rézk
33 þá í sveit meþ konum þeim helgum es vǫ́ru í fǫrunauti Pétrs postola, en þeygi vissu menn of stundar sakar hver hon var.

En stundu síþarr kómu þeir Petrus ok Clemens skipi sínu viþ Kípr.

36 Þar vǫ́ru þeir í hǫfn nøkkverri eigi allskamma stund. En þar gekk Petrus

30 Petres

'What do you expect, will any benefit come to me if I come to see the Apostle Peter?'

They answered: 'If you are truly in need, and moreover are willing to believe in Jesus Christ, the Son of God, then you will certainly receive grace through meeting him like all those who without deceit wish to hear and accept his teachings.'

The next day Mathidia went by their direction to see the Apostle Peter and fell at his feet and begged alms from him. Peter said:

'Why do you, a woman who is not sick, as far as I can see, now need to receive gifts of alms?'

She answered: 'My lady is ill and has leprosy, and I work to provide for us both. For that reason I am asking you for alms.'

Peter said: 'Why should you have to work for this woman?'

When Mathidia had to explain this, then she was greatly affected and was lost for words. Then the Apostle Peter said:

'It is my belief that you must have been a woman held in high regard and wealthy, and now you are recalling your former life and you are now ashamed of your wretchedness and the misery which has now come upon you.'

Mathidia said: 'There you are right, my lord,' said Mathidia to the Apostle.

Peter said: 'Let your lady come here, and we shall see what happens then.'

Then this was done that her lady was brought there to see the Apostle Peter, and she was laid at the feet of the Apostle. Then he said to both of them:

'Will you believe in God the Father Almighty and in his Son our Lord Jesus Christ and in the Holy Ghost?'

They answered: 'We will indeed believe what you preach.'

Then Peter made the sign of the cross over the sick woman and immediately she was cured of her leprosy. And next they were both baptised in the name of the Trinity. Then the woman who had been cured went to her family with the Apostle Peter's permission. Mathidia began to ask that she should be allowed to follow the Apostle Peter and she desired to hear his teachings daily, and moreover this was granted to her. She then joined the group of holy women who were in the Apostle Peter's company, but yet for the time being people did not know at all who she was.

And some time later Peter and Clement brought their ship to Cyprus. They were there in a certain harbour for quite a long time. And the Apostle

postoli upp á land hvern dag ok baþsk þar firir lǫngum á biargi nøkkveru
es nær var hǫfninni. Þar var ok vatnfall mikit einum megin hiá biargi
3   því. Þar kom af landi ofan at gangandi karl gamall ok hæruskeggi. En
hann stóþ þriá daga alla miǫk svá í sǫmum sporum, ok hlýddi til
bœnahalds postolans ok til formælis þess es hann veitti þeim mǫnnum
6   es til hans kómu. Karl sá mælti ekki orþ á þeim þrim dǫgum, en at aptni
ins þriþia dags, þá er hann biósk braut at ganga, þá mælti hann þessi orþ
of Pétr postola ok of fǫruneyti hans:
9   'Þessir eru menn góþir ok staþfastir í skaphǫfnum sínum ok munu
vera eigi vitrir at því [es mer vir]þisk.'
Þau orþ heyrþi Petrus ok mælti viþ sína menn: 'Takiþ ér karl þann ok
12 fœriþ mér!'
Þeir tóku karl þann síþan ok fœrþu honum. Þá mælti Petrus:
'Hverr er þú firir þér, fóstri?'
15 Hann svaraþi: 'Ek emk varþkarl einn fátœkr ok rúmverskr at kyni.'
Petrus mælti: 'Hvaþan af kallar ⟨þú⟩ oss menn góþa ok geþfasta ok
þó óvitra?'
18 Karl ok svaraþi: 'Því kalla ek yþr góþa ok geþfasta at ek heyrþa hvé
lítillátliga ok hvé óhrapalliga ér mæltuzk firir viþ Guþ yþvarn. Þat má
ek ok skilia af málsendum yþrum at ér elskiþ ráþvendi ok gœzku en ér
21 hatiþ ódáþir ok illsku. En af því kalla ek yþr óvitra menn at mér virþisk
svá sem ér kalliþ mann einn dauþan vera Guþ yþvarn ok trúiþ ér á hann
sem á Guþ. En þat má hverr maþr vitr skilia at einn es Guþ omnipotens
24 ok óbrigþligr.'
Petrus mælti: 'Þú kallar oss óvitra menn firir því at vér trúum á mann
dauþan. En ek kann þér þat segia at hvártki þú né annarr maþr má alvitr
27 vera nema hann skili þat at sá inn sami maþr es þú kallar dauþan, ok vér
trúum á, es bæþi maþr dauþligr ok Guþ lifandi omnipotens ok óbrigþligr.'
Karl mælti: 'Hversu meguþ ér slíkt satt vinna ófróþir menn ok íþrótta-
30 lausir?'
Petrus mælti: 'Þat vil ek at þú dvelisk meþ oss nøkkveria stund of daga
ok mon ek fá mann til af liþi mínu ok fǫruneyti at reyna íþróttir þínar.'
33 Karl mælti: 'Gørþu svá, ef þú vill.'
Annan dag eptir lét Petrus Clementem koma til máls viþ karl þann
firir því at hann þótti algerr at sér of allar íþróttir þær er Rúmverium
36 vǫru tíþar at kunna. Þá tóku þeir Clemens ok karl sá inn gamli at kannask

8 Pétrs   10 words supplied by Unger

Peter went ashore there each day and prayed there for a long time on a certain cliff which was close to the harbour. There was also a big river on one side by that cliff. An old man with a hoary beard came walking down there from inland. And he stood for three entire days almost on the same spot and listened to the Apostle's prayers and to the preaching which he gave to the people who came to him. The old man spoke not a word during those three days, but on the evening of the third day, when he started to go away, then he spoke these words about the Apostle Peter and his companions:

'These are good men and steadfast in their minds but cannot be wise, as it seems to me.'

Peter heard these words and spoke to his men: 'Take hold of that old man and bring him to me!'

They then took the old man and brought him to him. Then Peter said: 'What sort of person are you, grandfather?'

He answered: 'I am a poor watchman, and Roman by birth.'

Peter said: 'Why do you call us good men and steadfast and yet not wise?'

And the old man answered: 'I call you good and steadfast because I heard how humbly and how unhurriedly you have prayed to your God. I can also understand from your language that you love uprightness and kindness but you hate misdeeds and evil. But I say you are not wise men because it seems to me that you claim a dead man to be your God, and you believe in him as in God. But every wise man must realise that there is only one almighty and immutable God.'

Peter said: 'You claim that we are not wise men because we believe in a dead man. But I can tell you this, that neither you nor any other man can be fully wise unless he understands this, that this same man whom you call dead, and we believe in, is both a mortal man and the living almighty and immutable God.'

The old man said: 'How can you ignorant and uneducated men prove this?'

Peter said: 'I will have you stay with us for some time each day and I will get a man from among my followers and companions to test your educational accomplishments.'

The old man said: 'Do so, if you wish.'

The next day Peter had Clement come and talk with the old man, because he was thought perfect in all those educational accomplishments which it was usual for Romans to know. Then Clement and the old man began to

viþ of íþróttir. En svá reyndisk at hvárrtveggi kunni allar íþróttir þær er
spekingar vǫru vanir at kunna í þann tíþ. Síþan løgþu þeir fram firir sik
3   inn fyrsta dag íþrótt þá er grammatica heitir, ok kennir hon hvé réttliga
skal at hveriu orþi kveþa ok hvé ǫll orþ hneigiask á latínu tungu. Þá
íþrótt fóru þeir alla ifir inn fyrsta dag. Annan dag tóku þeir þá íþrótt at
6   rannsaka er rhetorica heitir, hon kennir málsnild alla. Inn þriþia dag
gekk fram dialectica es þrætur kann skilia. Inn fiorþa dag fóru þeir ifir
musicam es sǫngsíþrótt er. Inn fimta dag var kǫnnuþ arithmetica es
9   tǫlvísi alla greiþir. Inn sétta dag gekk fram geometria er kennir hvé
mæla skal hæþ eþa dýpt, lengþ eþa breidd vel hvers hlutar. Svá kannaþisk
til at allar íþróttir þær kunni sá inn gamli karl nekkvi framarr en Clemens,
12   ok kunnu þeir þó báþir vel. En [síþarst] tóku þeir at rœþa of stiǫrnuíþrótt
es astrono*m*ia heitir. E[n þ]ó vildi inn gamli karl eyvit láta a*t* leiþask at
rœþa of þá íþróttina. Þat fann Clemens ok mælti viþ hann:
15   'Hvárt er at þ*ú* kant verr þessa íþrótt en aþrar eþa hví lætr þú þér hér
svá fátt um finnask?'
Karl svaraþi: 'Þa íþrótt þóttumk ek bazt kunna, en þat hefir mér miǫk
18   brugþizk ok þykiumk ek nú mega ǫngu treystask of íþróttir mínar.'
Clemens mælti: 'Í hví hefir þér þat mest brugþizk?'
Karl svaraþi: 'Þat tregar mik miǫg at segia.'
21   Þá tók Clemens miǫk at grafa þat mál viþ hann. Enda var þá Petrus
postoli hiá málstefnu þeira, ok krafþi hann at sá inn gamli maþr skyldi
segia hvat ifir hann hafþi gengit. En honum þótti svá mikit firir at rifia
24   upp harm sinn allan þann es hann þóttisk be*þ*it hafa, ok kom hann trautt
orþi upp. En þá mælti hann of síþir:
'Ek átta mér konu góþa ok ráþvanda at því es ek ætlaþa, ok óttum vit
27   okkr þriá sonu. En hon villtisk ǫll frá mér ok lagþi hon illt firir sik. En
bróþir minn sannaþi þat firir mér af stiǫrnuíþrótt at stiǫrnugangr hafþi
sá verit á burþartíþ hennar at eigi væri vón at hon mætti ráþvǫnd vera til
30   elli sinnar. Síþan hefi ek allr firirorþit mik, enda trúi ek nú ekki á
stiǫrnuíþróttina síþan.'
Petrus mælti: 'Þat er villa mikil es þú ætlaþir at stiǫrnugangr myndi
33   ráþa ráþvendi konu þinnar. Þat hygg ek at þú munt þat rétt hafa ætlat es
þú hugþir konu þína góþa konu vera ok ráþvanda. Segþu nú mér sannliga
alla athǫfn þína ok má vera at þat verþi þér at nekkverri huggun.'

6 rethorica   12–13 *word and letters supplied by Unger*   13 astronoua . . . af
15 þau   24 boþit

make their acquaintance with each other's accomplishments. And so it turned out that each of them had all the accomplishments which philosophers usually knew at that time. Then on the first day they demonstrated the art which is called grammar, and it teaches how one should pronounce each word correctly and how all words are declined in the Latin language. The first day they went over the whole of that subject. The second day they began to examine the art which is called rhetoric, it teaches every kind of eloquence. The third day it was the turn of logic which can resolve disputes. The fourth day they went over music which is the art of singing. The fifth day arithmetic was explored which deals with all matters of computation. The sixth day it was the turn of geometry which teaches how to measure the height or depth, length or breadth of almost everything. So it became evident that the old man knew all these arts somewhat better than Clement, and yet they both knew them well. And finally they began to discuss the subject of stars, which is called astronomy. But yet the old man would by no means be brought to discuss that subject. Clement noticed this and said to him:

'Is it because you know this subject worse than others, or why have you so little to say about it?'

The old man answered: 'I thought I knew this subject best, but it has failed me badly and I think I cannot now trust anything in my accomplishments.'

Clement said: 'How has it failed you most?'

The old man answered: 'It grieves me much to say.'

Then Clement began to probe into the matter with him. And moreover the Apostle Peter was then present at their discussion, and he begged that the old man should say what had happened to him. But he found it so hard to go over all the trouble he felt he had suffered that he could scarcely utter a word. And then at last he said:

'I had a good and upright woman for my wife, as I thought, and we had three sons. And she was led astray from me completely and she took to wicked ways. But my brother proved to me by astronomy that the course of the stars had been such at the time of her birth that there was no likelihood that she would stay upright till her old age. After that I entirely lost confidence, and moreover since then I now have no faith in astronomy.'

Peter said: 'It is a great error that you thought that the course of the stars would govern your wife's uprightness. I think this, that you thought right when you believed your wife to be a good and upright woman. Tell me now truly about all you have done and it may be that that will be some comfort to you.'

Þá mælti hann sá inn gamli karl: 'Ek heiti Faustinianus en kona mín hét Mathidia, sonr minn es Clemens.'

3　Þá tók Clemens viþ at vakna ok at heilsa fǫþur sínum ok varþ þar fagnafundr mikill meþ þeim feþgum. En því næst kom þat upp at þar var Mathidia í fǫruneyti þeira Pétrs postola, ok þar vǫru synir þeira

6　Faustus ok Faustinus es þá kǫlluþusk Niceta ok Aquila. Þá verþr hvert þeira friþgina ǫþru fegit ok sǫgþusk sín á milli allt þat es ifir þau hafþi gengit síþan er þau hǫfþu skilizk. En eptir þat talþi Petrus postoli trú

9　firir Faustiniano ok beiddi at hann myndi skírn taka. En hann svaraþi: 'Ek vil trúa sicut þú kennir, en svá fremi vil ek skírn taka es ek emk nekkvi fróþari at helgum ritningum en ek siá enn.'

12　Þá réþsk Faustinianus til fǫruneytis meþ Petro postola ok gerþisk honum svá hlýþinn ok svá hendilangr sem hann væri honum í barnœsku til læringar seldr. Hann hafþi þá virþing mikla af ǫllum mǫnnum þeim

15　es Petro fylgþu þótt hann bærisk ipse lítit á.

Í þann tíþ spurþi Petrus postoli at Símon inn illi, es magus var kallaþr, villti þióþ alla í Antiochia svát þeir trúþu hann at sǫnnu goþ vera, en

18　þeir kǫstuþu niþr trú þeiri allri es Petrus hafþi kennt þeim. Þá fýstisk Petrus at fara þingat, enda fór hann unz hann kom í borg þá á Iórsalalandi es Cesarea heitir. Þar hafþi Cornelius hundraþshǫfþingi vald mikit, sá

21　er Petrus hafþi skírþan. Hann veitti þar viþtekiu góþa Petro postola ok hann fekk honum ríþerasveit mikla til fǫrunautis í Anþekiu. En er þeir nálguþusk þingat þá spurþu þeir at borgarmenninir ætluþu at banna Petro

24　inngǫngu í borgina Anþekiu af firirtǫlum Símonar ins illa. Þá mælti Faustinianus viþ Petar postola:

'Theophilus heitir maþr gǫfugr í Anþekiu. Hann hefir opt verit gestr

27　minn í Rúmaborg. Ek hefi ok iamnan verit at herbergi í húsum hans þá er ek hafþak veldi of heruþum þessum ok var vinátta okkur einka góþ. Nú vil ek fara til fundar viþ hann ok mun ek taka herbergi at hans. En

30　þaþan af vætti ek at vit munum svá umb sýsla at þú munt ná inngǫngu í borgina ok fǫruneyti þit.'

Petrus mælti: 'Farþu ef þú vill, en þó fýsi ek þik at þú takir áþr skírn.

33　Þá vætti ek at Símon myni ekki mega þér til meins gera þótt it finnizk, en ella es mér vón at hann geri þér nekkvert ógagn eþa geig.'

Faustinianus mælti: 'Ekki mein mon hann of gera. Þá vil ek skírn

36　taka er ek køm aptr til þín.'

7 friþgina] *Unger emends to* feþgina 'parents'　21 góþar　27 iamnat

Then the old man said: 'I am called Faustinianus and my wife was called Mathidia, my son is Clement.'

Then Clement began to realise and to greet his father and there was a joyful meeting between father and son. And next it turned out that Mathidia was there among the Apostle Peter's company, and their sons Faustus and Faustinus were there, who then were calling themselves Niceta and Aquila. Then each member of the family rejoiced in the other and talked between themselves of all that had happened to them since they had parted. And after that the Apostle Peter preached the Faith to Faustinianus and asked him to receive baptism. But he replied:

'I will believe whatever you teach, but I will accept baptism only when I am somewhat more learned in the Holy Scriptures than I am now.'

Then Faustinianus joined company with the Apostle Peter, and he became as obedient and as helpful as if he had been handed over to him to educate in his childhood. He then had great esteem from all the people who followed Peter, though he himself bore himself humbly.

At that time the Apostle Peter heard that Simon the Evil, who was called Magus, deceived all the people in Antioch so that they believed him to be truly a god, and they abandoned all the Faith which Peter had taught them. Then Peter became eager to go there, and moreover he travelled until he reached the city in Palestine which is called Cesarea. The centurion Cornelius, whom Peter had baptised, had great authority there. He gave the Apostle Peter a good reception and provided him with a large company of mounted soldiers to accompany him to Antioch. And when they drew near there then they heard that the citizens were going to prevent Peter entering the city of Antioch at the instigation of Simon the Evil. Then Faustinianus said to the Apostle Peter:

'There is a nobleman in Antioch called Theophilus. He has often been my guest in Rome. I have also always lodged in his house when I was in charge of these districts and our friendship was especially close. Now I will go to see him and I will take lodgings at his house. And after that I expect that the two of us will manage it so that you and your company will gain entry to the city.'

Peter said: 'Go if you wish, but yet I urge you to be baptised first. I hope then that Simon will not be able to do you any harm even if you meet each other, but otherwise I think it likely that he will do you some hurt or injury.'

Faustinianus said: 'He will do no harm. I am willing to be baptised when I return to you.'

Petrus mælti: 'Verþi sem Guþ vill.'

Síþan fór Faustinianus til Anþekiu ok tók Theophilus vel viþ honum.

3 Hann hafþi fá daga þar verit áþr hann gat snúit Theophilo frá ǫllum
trúnaþi viþ Símon ok tók hann upp trú rétta sicut Petrus postoli hafþi
kennt honum fyrr meirr.

6 Svá barsk at einn hvern dag at þeir Faustinianus ok Símon gengusk
at móti á stræti ok sá hvárr þeira annan, en ekki mæltusk þeir viþ.
Faustinianus þóttisk kenna blæ nekkvern á andliti sér es þeir gingusk at
9 móti *svá* sem orpit væri bleytu nøkkverri í andlit honum. En litlu síþarr
kom hann í herbergi sitt ok hugþisk ekki hafa skipask at ifirlitum sínum.
En hann var þó orþinn svá glíkr Símoni at ásiá at engi mátti maþr ǫþrum
12 glíkari vera en Faustinianus var Símoni, ok eigi kenndu menn hvárn þeira
sǫ́. En þegar es hann kom í herbergi þá kallaþi Th⟨e⟩ophilus ok mælti:
'Dragstu út heþan diǫfuls maþr! Engva dvǫl skaltu hér hafa!'
15 Faustinianus mælti: 'Hví kveþr þú mik svá hermiliga, húsbúandi?'
Theophilus mælti: 'Ætlar þú at ek vita eigi hverr þú ert firir þér, Símon
inn illi ok inn fiǫlkunngi?'
18 Faustinianus mælti: 'Faustinianus em ek en eigi Símon inn illi.'
Theophilus mælti: 'Annan máttu svá blekkia en eigi mik. Ek kenni
þik fullgerla hverr þú ert.'
21 Faustinianus mælti: 'Hyggþu at fatabúningi mínum ok klæþum, ok kenn
mik þaþan af ef þú mátt mik eigi at ifirlitum kenna eþa ásiónu minni.'
Sem trauþast mátti hann því til sanns koma firir Theophilo at hann væri
24 eigi Símon magus. En er þeir þóttusk siá báþir hvaþan af hann hafþi mein
fingit þá réþu þeir þat at hann fór á braut ór borginni sem skiótast ok á fund
Pétrs postola. En er hann kom þar þá fell hann til fóta postolanum ok mælti:
27 'Veittu mér miskunn, herri minn,' kvaþ Faustinianus, 'ok lát mik
hafa ifirlit mín, þau sem ek hafþa áþr Símon spillti ásiónu minni.'
Petrus postoli svaraþi: 'Ekki sýnisk mér brugþit vera ifirlitum þínum.
30 En þótt ǫþrum mǫnnum sýnisk brugþit vera ásiónu þinni þá er þér þat
ekki mein.'
Faustinianus mælti: 'Hverr maþr hyggr mik inn versta mann vera, sá
33 er mik sér.'
Petrus mælti: 'Þat it sama skal Símoni verþa at miklu hlœgi es hann
þykisk þér hafa til meins gert. Fylgþu nú ráþum mínum,' kvaþ Petrus.

---

6 Faustinusianus   9 ne   16 'hʀ|veʀ' *over line break.*

Peter said: 'Let it be as God wills!'

Then Faustinianus went to Antioch and Theophilus welcomed him. He had stayed there only a few days before he was able to turn Theophilus from all faith in Simon, and he adopted the true faith as the Apostle Peter had taught him formerly.

It happened thus one day that Faustinianus and Simon met each other in the street and each saw the other, but they did not speak to each other. Faustinianus thought he felt a puff of wind on his face when they met each other as though something wet was splashed on his face. And a little later he came into his lodging and thought that he had not changed in appearance. But he had, however, become so like Simon to look at that no man could be more like another than Faustinianus was to Simon, and people did not know which of them they were looking at. And when he went into his lodging, then Theophilus shouted and said:

'Get out of here, servant of the Devil! You shall not stay here!'

Faustinianus asked: 'Why do you greet me so angrily, landlord?'

Theophilus said: 'Do you think that I do not know what sort of person you are, Simon the Evil and the Mage?'

Faustinianus said: 'I am Faustinianus and not Simon the Evil.'

Theophilus said: 'You may impose upon another thus, but not me. I know full well who you are.'

Faustinianus said: 'Look at my apparel and clothes, and know me from those if you cannot recognise me from my appearance or countenance.'

Only with the greatest difficulty could he convince Theophilus that he was not Simon Magus. But when they both realised the source of the harm done to him, then they arranged it so that he went out of the city as fast as possible and to see the Apostle Peter. And when he came there he fell at the feet of the Apostle and said:

'Have mercy on me, my lord,' said Faustinianus, 'and let me have back my appearance, which I had before Simon corrupted my countenance.'

The Apostle Peter answered: 'It does not seem to me that your appearance has changed. And even if your appearance seems changed to other people, still that does you no harm.'

Faustinianus said 'Every man who sees me believes that I am the most evil man.'

Peter said: 'The very fact that Simon thinks he has done you harm shall bring great ridicule down on him. Follow my advice now,' said Peter.

'Tak þú nú blezun af mér ok far síþan í Anþekiu ok í hús Theophili
vinar þíns, ok lát þar ekki verþa vart viþ þik fyrr en þú gengr þar fram á
3 stræti einn hvern dag þá er þar er fiǫlmenni mikit. Þú skal þá kallask
vera Símon magus. Þú skal teliask verþa skyldr til þess of sinn á hveriu
ári at lýsa siþu þína ok atgiǫrvi firir alþýþu. Síþan skaltu segia á hǫnd
6 þér fiǫlkyngi ok allar flærþir illar þær er ek kann þér segia at Símon es
saþr at. Þess vætti ek at Símon mon koma at heyra á orþ þín. Hann mon
eigi mega standask tǫlu þína þessa. Hann mon ráþa til menn sína at
9 skióta at þér eþa gera þér nekkvern geig [ef þeir megu]. Þú skal hafa áþr
ráþna til tvá menn at halda firir þik skiǫldum ok hlífa þér ef menn veita
þér tilráþ. En ef þér verþa tilráþ veitt þá kostaþu at hverfa áþr á braut ór
12 borginni sem skiótast ok kom síþan til mín.'
      En eptir þessa tilskipun tók Faustinianus blezun af Petro ok fór síþan
í Anþekiu ok háttaþi ǫllu sicut Petrus bauþ honum. En er þar kom at
15 hann stóþ á stræti ok talþisk Símon vera ok lýsti ifir ódáþum sínum ok
endemum þá máttisk Símon magus þat eigi of standask. Hann lét skióta
at honum ǫrum tvennum. En þar brugþu menn skiǫldum viþ es til vǫru
18 settir at hlífa Faustiniano. Þá kallaþi Faustinianus ok mælti:
      'Nú mon ek hætta þessi rœþu en þvísa næst mon ek sýnask meþal
yþvar á stræti.'
21   Viþ þessi orþ hvarf hann á braut allr svát hann varþ hvergi litinn í
borginni þaþan frá. En lýþr sá er áþr hafþi horft á hann litaþisk umb ok
só þeir þá Símon standa á meþal sín. Þá tóku þeir at rækia hann ok
24 mæltu viþ hann:
      'Nú vitum vér hverr svikari þú ert. Hefir þú nú ipse sagt eptir þér undr
ok endemi þau es engu megu viþ iamnask.'
27   En er hann vildi ipse svara firir sik þá œstisk ǫll alþýþa á hendr honum
ok kǫstuþu þeir at honum grióti ok trióm ok hvívetna es þeir móttu til
fá. Í þeiri rimmu róku þeir borgarmenn Símon inn illa á braut ór Anþekiu
30 svát hann efldisk þar ekki síþan of aldr.
      Faustinianus kom brátt á fund Pétrs postola ok sagþi honum þau tíþendi
es gerzk hǫfþu í Antiochia, ok lét hann þess vón at hann myndi þar fá
33 góþar viþtǫkur. En síþan sendi Petrus postoli Nicetam ok Aquilam í
Anþekiu at gera vart viþ at hann var þingat á fǫr. En er borgarlýþrinn
vissi at Pétr postoli nólgaþisk þingat þá fóru allir inir gǫfgustu menn

9 *words supplied by* Unger   16 endeminum

'Receive now my blessing and then go into Antioch and into the house of your friend Theophilus, and do not let anyone know you are there until you go out onto the street one day when there is a large crowd. You shall then claim to be Simon Magus. You shall declare yourself bound once each year to proclaim your practices and accomplishments to the people. Then you must confess to sorcery and all the evil deceits which I can tell you that Simon is guilty of. I expect that Simon will come and listen to your words. He will not be able to tolerate this speech of yours. He will get his men to shoot at you or do you some injury if they can. You must previously have arranged for two men to hold shields in front of you and to protect you if men attack you. And if you are attacked then try to get away from the city as fast as possible and then come to me.'

And after this instruction Faustinianus received Peter's blessing and then went into Antioch and fixed everything just as Peter had told him to. And when it came about that he stood on the street and said that he was Simon and proclaimed his misdeeds and monstrous acts, then Simon Magus could not put up with that. He had two volleys of arrows shot at him. But men who were charged to protect Faustinianus warded them off with shields. Then Faustinianus shouted and said:

'Now I will cease this talk and next I will appear among you in the street.'

With these words he disappeared completely so that he was never seen in the city from then on. And the crowd who had previously had their eyes on him looked around and then they saw Simon standing among them. They began then to reject him and said to him:

'Now we know what a deceiver you are. You yourself have now informed on yourself of shameful deeds and monstrous acts which are unparalleled.'

But when he wanted to defend himself then all the people became furious with him and they threw at him stones and sticks and whatever they could get hold of. In the tumult the citizens drove Simon the Evil away out of Antioch so that he made no headway there ever after.

Faustinianus soon came to see the Apostle Peter and told him the news of what had happened in Antioch, and he said it was likely that he would have a good reception there. And then the Apostle Peter sent Niceta and Aquila into Antioch to make it known that he was on his way there. And when the citizens learnt that the Apostle Peter was approaching there, then all the most distinguished men went a long way out of the city to

langt á braut ór borginni á mót Petro ok gingu berfœttir ok í hárklæþum,
ok sýndu svá iþrun sína Petro postola firir þat es þeir hǫfþu horfit eptir
3 villu Símonar ins illa ok trúat á flærþir hans ok illsku.

Þá er Petrus kom í borgina þá dreif at honum alþýþa manns ok vǫru
þar bornir at honum siúkir menn ýmisligum sóttum hvaþan æva, þeir er
6 sér vættu happs ok heilsu af verþleikum postolans ok iarteinum hans.
Þá leit Petrus ifir fólk þat es til hans var komit ok þakkaþi [Guþi] t[rú]
þ[ei]ra [þá er hann sá algerva], es þá var komin í brióst þeim. Síþan
9 mælti Petrus postoli viþ lýþinn:

'Þat meguþ ér siá at ek em maþr glíkr yþr at ǫllu øþli ok at óstyrkleik
líkama míns. Nú skuluþ ér eigi þat hyggia at ek mega gefa yþr heilsu af
12 krapti mínum. En ef ér iátiþ því at Iesus Christus, filius Domini lifanda,
gefr yþr heilsu ok trúiþ ér á hann af ǫllum hug, þá er vǫn at ér megiþ
miskunn fá í hans namni.'

15 Þá iátti allr lýþr Christo Domino ok lézk búinn vera at gera þat allt es
Petrus vildi bióþa. En í því bili kom liós mikit af himni ofan ifir allan
lýþ, enda fingu þá þeir menn allir bót meina sinna es siúkir hǫfþu verit.
18 Þá runnu krypplingar at fótum Petro postola ok ǫll alþýþa lofaþi nomen
Christi Domini. En þaþan frá fylgþi svá mikill Guþs kraptr Petro postola
at á siau dǫgum inum næstum tóku tíu þúsundir manna skírn meþ fullri
21 trú til Guþs.

Eptir þat beiddi Theophilus inn kristnasti maþr í Antiochia Petar
postola at hann vígþi hǫll gǫfugliga es hann átti til kirkiu, enda fór þat
24 fram. Í þeiri kirkiu var settr stóll Pétrs postola á þeim degi sem nú er
síþan haldin Pétrsmessa á vár, ok þá sǫng þar Pétr postoli fyrstr messu
allra manna at því er bœkr segia. Á þeim degi fell Faustinianus til fóta
27 Pétrs postola firir allri alþýþu ok mælti þessi orþ:

'Nú þykia mér Guþs orþ þau er þú hefir sagt í brióst mér vera búin til
at gera góþan ávǫxt. Nú fýsumk ek at taka skírn ok vil ek síþan vera
30 hluttakeri heilagrar þiónustu.'

Þá skírþi Petrus Faustinianum ok þá tók hann ásiónu sína þá sem
hann hafþi haft áþr Símon brygþi ifirlitum hans. Á þeim degi talþi Petrus
33 lengi firir lýþnum ok hóf þar mál sitt es Faustinianus var, ok gaf á honum
dœmi ǫþrum mǫnnum hvé hann var snúinn frá heiþnum dómi af miskunn Guþs til algǫrrar trú ok til dýrligs lífs. En þaþan frá virþi alþýþa

7–8 words supplied by Unger

meet Peter and walked barefoot and in hair shirts, and in this way showed their repentance to the Apostle Peter for having followed the heresy of Simon the Evil and believed in his deceits and wickedness.

When Peter entered the city, then all the people flocked to him and men sick with various diseases, who looked for good fortune and health from the merits of the Apostle and his miracles, were carried to him there from every direction. Then Peter looked over the people who had come to him and thanked God for their faith which he saw perfectly had then entered their breasts. Then the Apostle Peter spoke to the people:

'You can see that I am a man like you in all my nature and in the infirmity of my body. Now you must not think that I can give you health by my own power. But if you acknowledge that Jesus Christ, the son of the living Lord, will give you health and you believe in him with all your mind, then it is likely that you may receive grace in his name.'

Then all the people acknowledged the Lord Christ and said that they were ready to do everything that Peter wished to command. And at that moment a great light came down from heaven over all the people, and moreover all those people who had been sick then received healing of their ailments. Then cripples ran to the feet of the Apostle Peter and all the people praised the name of the Lord Christ. And from then on such great power of God was in the Apostle Peter that in the following seven days ten thousand people were baptised with complete faith in God.

After that Theophilus, the most Christian person in Antioch, asked the Apostle Peter to consecrate a magnificent hall which he was using as a church, and moreover this took place. The throne of the Apostle Peter was set up in that church on the day which now is held as the feast day of St Peter in the spring, and then the Apostle Peter sang mass there the first of all men according to what books say. On that day Faustinianus fell down at the feet of the Apostle Peter before all the people and spoke these words:

'Now the words of God which you have spoken and put into my breast seem to me to be ready to bear good fruit. Now I am eager to receive baptism and I wish afterwards to be a partaker of the Holy Sacrament.'

Then Peter baptised Faustinianus and he then recovered his countenance which he had had before Simon changed his appearance. On that day Peter preached for a long time to the people and began his sermon with Faustinianus, and made of him an example to other people how he was turned from heathendom by the grace of God to perfect faith and to a glorious life. And from then on the ordinary people regarded Faustinianus

Faustinianum sem engil Guþs ok margir menn þiónuþu honum ekki
miþr en Petro postola. Ævi hans lauksk meþ góþu ok konu hans ok suna
3 í trú heilagri ok atferþ dýrligri at Guþs vilia.

VI

Petrus postoli helt siau vetr byskupstól í Anþekiu, en síþan kom hann til
Rúmaborgar á þeim dǫgum er Claudius var keiseri ifir ǫllum heimi. Þar
6 var hann fyrstr páfi ok hafþi hann þat veldi hálfan þriþia tøg vetra.
Clemens fylgþi honum miǫk svá alla ævi þaþan frá er hann kom til
fundar viþ Pétr postola, ok Clemens gerþi bók þá of farahag ok iarteinir
9 Pétrs postola es heitir It⟨in⟩erarium Petri, en þat þýþisk sem sé farabók
Pétrs. Svá segir bók at á ofanverþum dǫgum Pétrs postola þá kom einn
hvern dag fiǫlþi manna á fund Pétrs postola at heyra formæli hans ok
12 kenning. Þá reis Petrus upp á mannfundi þeim inum fiǫlmenna ok tók
hann hǫnd Clemens ok mælti síþan:
       'Þat hefir Dominus vitrat mér at nú nólgask miǫk andlátstíþ mín. Nú
15 set ek þenna mann Clementem í stól minn at stýra ok at ráþa allri
Rúmaborgar kristni, ok honum býþ ek at halda upp kenningum helgum
ok boþorþum Guþs ǫllum eptir dag minn meþ veldi því es ek hefi tekit
18 af lærifeþr mínum ok Domino Iesu Christo at binda ok leysa allt þat es
ek vil á himni ok á iǫrþu. Siá maþr hefir mér fylgt miǫk langa ævi vel
ok trúliga, ok veit ek hann bazt til fallinn at sitia í stóli mínum firir trú
21 sakar ok vitrleiks ok gœzku.'
       Þá setti hann Clementem í stól sinn ok lagþi hendr sínar í hǫfuþ honum
meþ blezun heilagri þeiri at hann vígþi hann til byskups ok til páfa ifir
24 allri kristni. Þá minnti Petrus páfi Clemens á miǫk mǫrgum orþum hversu
hann sky⟨l⟩di halda byskupdóm, eþa hvé hann skildi stýra kristni þeiri
es hann var þá ifir settr.
27   Þaþan frá leiþ eigi langt skeiþ unz Guþs unnandi Petrus postoli lét líf
sitt firir ina háleitustu ǫst viþ inn almáttka Guþ sicut ipse Dominus hafþi
vitrat honum. Inn fyrsti páfi af Petro vígþr ok til kørinn var Linus ok var
30 hann litla stund. En annarr páfi var Cletus eptir Linum at forráþi Pétrs
postola ok lifþi skamma stund. Inn þriþi páfi frá Petro var siá inn gǫfgi
Clemens, sonr Faustinianus ins mesta spekings, ok hann var sonr Math*i*die
33 innar kynstœrstu konu ok dásamliga ráþvandrar sicut fyrr var frá sagt.

32 Mathadie

as an angel of God and many men paid homage to him no less than to the Apostle Peter. His life and that of his wife and sons ended well in holy faith and in splendid conduct in accordance with God's will.

VI

The Apostle Peter held the bishop's see in Antioch for seven years, and then he came to Rome in the days when Claudius was emperor over the whole world. He was the first pope there and he had that authority for twenty-five years. Clement was with him almost all his life from the time when he went to see the Apostle Peter, and Clement wrote the book on the journeys and miracles of the Apostle Peter which is called 'Itinerarium Petri', and that means as it were 'Peter's book of travels'.* A book says that towards the end of the Apostle Peter's days a multitude of people came to see the Apostle Peter on a certain day to hear his preaching and teaching. Then Peter stood up at that crowded meeting and he took Clement's hand and then said:

'The Lord has revealed to me that the time of my death now draws very close. Now I set this man Clement in my throne to govern and to rule all the Church in Rome, and I command him to uphold all the holy teachings and commandments of God after my day with the authority which I have received from my Teacher and Lord Jesus Christ to bind and to loose whatever I will in Heaven and on Earth. This man has followed me well and faithfully for a very long time, and I know that he is best fitted to sit in my throne because of his faith and wisdom and goodness.'

Then he seated Clement in his throne and placed his hands on his head with the sacred benediction of consecrating him bishop and pope over the whole of Christendom. Then Pope Peter reminded Clement in very many words how he should carry out his episcopal duties, and how he should govern the Church which he was then put in charge of.

From then not a long time passed until the Apostle Peter, lover of God, lost his life on account of his sublime love for Almighty God as the Lord himself had revealed to him. The first pope consecrated by Peter and elected was Linus and he was pope for a little while. And the second pope after Linus under the guardianship of the Apostle Peter was Cletus and he lived for a short time. The third pope from Peter was the noble Clement, son of Faustinianus the very great philosopher, and he was the son of Mathidia, the most nobly born woman and wonderfully upright as was told above.

---

* Traditionally an alternative name for the *Recognitiones*. The 'book' quoted next is considered to be a source of the *Epistula Clementis ad Iacobum* (see p. xix above).

VII

En siá inn helgi ættarbœtir, Clemens, glíkþi atferþ sína ok kenningar
helgar eptir Petro postola lærifeþr sínum, ok Clemens páfi hafþi ǫst ok
3 elsku mikla af Gyþingum ok heiþnum mǫnnum sicut af kristnu fólki.
Heiþnir menn elskuþu Clemens af því at hann fœldi eigi siþ þeira, heldr
sýndi hann þeim meþ mikilli skynsemi af þeira bókum siálfra hversu
6 illa ok flærþsamliga þeir Þórr eþa Óþinn eþa aþrir æsir vǫru getnir, ok
hversu illa ok herfiliga þeir lifþu ok dó síþan vesalliga heþan ór heimi,
ok má þá af því at ǫngum sannǫndum goþ kalla. Clemens páfi sagþi svá
9 heiþnum mǫnnum at þeir mǫndi þegar ǫþlask líkn ok miskunn af Guþi
es þeir hyrfi frá blótum ok allri gǫfgun viþ skurþgoþ sín. En Gyþingar
elskuþu Clemens páfa af því at hann lét vel of lǫgum þeira ok talþi
12 langfeþr þeira vera helga menn ok Guþs vini mikla, ok kvaþ eigi myndu
aþra fyrr ǫþlask ok eignask inngǫngu himinríkis vistar ef þeir trýþi því
es helgir spámenn þeira hǫfþu spát ok firirsagt of hingatkomu Christ*i*
15 Domini í heim þenna. En af heilagri vitru ok Guþi gefinni ok hyggiligri
ráþleitni teygþi Clemens páfi Gyþinga ok heiþna menn til ásthúþar viþ
inn almáttka Guþ Fǫþur ok Son ok Helgan Anda þann er bæþi er einn
18 ok þrír, ok fekk svá umb rœtt viþ allan lýþ at sem sízt stygþisk hugr
þeira viþ kenningar hans, ok svát ǫllum rynni sem mest ástarhugr til
heilagrar misericordie eingetins sonar Guþs. En eigi hafþi hann þessi
21 blíþmæli firir þeim sǫkum viþ lýþinn at hann hræddisk ógnir manna né
styriǫld firir því at Clemens boþaþi þar namn Guþs ok trú rétta es hann
vissi áþr mesta heiþni vera ok skurþgoþavillu.
24   Ok af hans kenningu snerisk til trú réttrar ágæt kona sú er Theodora
hét ok kom opt til kirkiu ok þiónaþi ástsamliga ok vel Guþi almáttkum.
En Sisinnius búandi hennar Theodoru var grimmr maþr ok heiþinn. En
27 einn hvern dag gekk Sisinnius af forvitnis sǫkum eptir Theodoru konu
sinni í ǫnnur kirkiudyrr. En er lærþir studdu bœn páfans ok kvǫþu amen
þá varþ Sisinnius þegar bæþi blindr ok daufr ok mælti svá viþ þióna
30 sína at þeir skyldi taka í hendr honum ok leiþa hann á braut þaþan,
'þvíat ek má nú hvártki siá né heyra.'
    Þiónar hans ok þrælar leiddu hann of kirkiuna innan ok móttu eigi
33 hitta út ok fundu eigi dyrr á kirkiunni. Þeir fóru svá opt í hring of kirkiuna
innan unz þeir kómu þar of síþir es Theodora var kona hans á bœnum

14 Christum

VII

So this blessed ornament of his family, Clement, modelled his conduct and holy teachings on his teacher the Apostle Peter, and Pope Clement won affection and deep love from Jews and heathens as well as from Christian people. Heathens loved Clement because he did not mock their faith, but rather demonstrated to them very rationally out of their own books how evilly and deceitfully Þórr and Óðinn and other gods had been begotten, and how wickedly and wretchedly they lived and then died miserably out of this world, and therefore they cannot be called gods on any truthful grounds. Pope Clement told heathen men this, that they would gain comfort and grace from God as soon as they abandoned sacrifices and all worship of their carven images. And the Jews loved Pope Clement because he expressed approval of their laws and said that their ancestors were holy men and great friends of God, and said that others could not sooner obtain and gain entry to life in the Kingdom of Heaven if they would believe what their holy prophets had foretold and prophesied about the coming of the Lord Christ into this world. And with his holy and God-given wisdom and with his prudent efforts Pope Clement drew Jews and heathens to love of the Almighty God, Father, Son, and Holy Ghost, who is both one and three, and managed to speak to all the people so that their hearts were offended by his teaching as little as possible, and so that the greatest possible love for the holy grace of God's only begotten son flowed into all of them. And he did not use these blandishments with the people because he feared men's threats or violence, for Clement preached the name of God and the true faith where he already knew the greatest heathendom and idolatry existed.

And from his teaching a woman of noble birth who was called Theodora turned to the true faith and came often to church and served Almighty God lovingly and well. But Sisinnius, the husband of this Theodora, was a fierce and heathen man. And one day out of curiosity Sisinnius followed his wife Theodora in by another church-door. And when the clergy endorsed the Pope's prayer and said Amen then Sisinnius at once became both blind and deaf, and spoke thus to his servants that they should take him by the hands and lead him away from there, 'because now I can neither see nor hear.'

His servants and slaves led him around inside the church but were not able to find their way out and found no doors in the church. Thus they went many times in a circle round the inside of the church until at last they came to where his wife Theodora was at her prayers. And when she

sínum. En er hon sá hvar þeir fóru meþ Sisinnium búanda hennar þá
veik hon fyrst frá fundi þeira, ok ætlaþi hon at Sisinnius møndi siá
3   nakkvat þvíat hann hóf upp augu sín sem heileygr maþr. En þó sendi
hon mann eptir þeim at vita þat hvat þeim væri orþit til meins es þeir
fóru svá ógreitt. En þeir svǫruþu ok sǫgþu svá:
6   'Þá er Sisinnius dominus várr vildi siá þá hluti ok heyra es honum var
eigi lofat, heiþnum manni ok trúlausum, þá týndi hann af því bæþi heyrn
sinni ok sýn, ok megu nú allir siá þat at vér hittum eigi leiþ óra ór kirkiu út.'
9   Theodora fell á kné til bœnar sinnar þá er hon heyrþi tíþendi þessi
sǫgþ ok baþ inn almáttka Guþ meþ tǫrum [at þeir] mætti ganga út ór
kirkiunni. Þá mælti Theodo[ra] viþ þrælana:
12   'Takiþ ér nú í hendr Sisinnio ok leiþiþ hann heim. En ek mon halda
svá bœn minni sem oss gegni ǫllum bazt ok skynda þegar heim es
tíþum es lokit.'
15   Sveinarnir tóku í hendr herra sínum Sisinnio sem Theodora bauþ þeim
ok leiddu heim til hallar sinnar. En þeir fóru síþan aptr til fundar viþ
Theodoru skyndiliga ok sǫgþu henni Sisinnium vera bæþi blindan ok
18 daufan. Þá hvarf Theodora af nýiu til bœnar sinnar ok baþ honum
þrásamliga Guþ misericordie búanda sínum, ok fell honum til fóta
Clemens páfa þegar er tíþum var lokit ok sagþi búanda sinn vera bæþi
21 blindan ok daufan, 'þá er hann vildi forvitnask of hagi okkra.'
    Þá felldi Clemens tǫr ok eggiaþi þá menn alla es þar vǫru at biþia firir
Sisinnio at Guþ gæfi honum sýn ok heyrn, ok fór hann heim meþ
24 Theodoru es bœn þeira var lokit ok hafþi hann allt traust undir Guþi
almáttkum. En hiú hans ǫll Sisinnius stóþu grátandi ifir honum, ok mátti
hann ekki til siá eþa heyra es hiú hans heilsuþu Clemens páfa ok
27 Theodoru. Þá hóf Clemens páfi upp augu sín til Domini ok baþ Sisinnio
misericordie a Domino ok mælti á þessa lund:
    'Dominus meus Iesus Christus, þú er gaf⟨t⟩ postola þínum Petari
30 himinríkis lukla, lærifeþr mínum ok meistera, ok þú heilagr Guþ mæltir
svá viþ hann at sá skal hverr leysask á iǫrþu frá ǫllum meinum ok ǫþlask
eilífa miskunn af Guþi feþr firir þitt heilagt árnaþarorþ ok himinríkis vist
33 er þú vill svá vera láta, en sá hverr bundinn ok fyrdœmþr ok Guþs flótta-
maþr verþa er þitt atkvæþi es þat, bióþþu nú Dominus at upp lúkisk augu
þessa manns ok eyru, þvíat þú mæltir svá: "Hverskis es ér biþiþ, trúiþ ér
36 því, kristnir menn, at ér munuþ geta þat es ér biþiþ, ok mun svá verþa."

10 words supplied by Unger   29 ert gaf

saw where they were going with her husband Sisinnius, then she turned away at first from encountering them, and thought that Sisinnius must be able to see a bit because he raised his eyes like a man of normal sight. But nevertheless she sent a man after them to find out what harm had befallen them since they moved so awkwardly. And they answered and said thus:

'When our Master Sisinnius wished to see and hear those things which were not permitted to him, being a heathen and an unbelieving man, then because of that he lost both his hearing and sight, and now all can see that we cannot find our way out of the church.'

Theodora fell to her knees in prayer when she heard about all this and with tears prayed to the Almighty God that they might get out of the church. Then Theodora said to the slaves:

'Now take Sisinnius by the hands and lead him home. But I will go on praying as will be best for us all and hurry home as soon as the service is finished.'

The lads took their master Sisinnius by the hands as Theodora told them and led him home to his hall. They then hurried back to meet Theodora and told her that Sisinnius was both blind and deaf. Then Theodora turned again to her prayers and begged God persistently for grace for her husband, and fell at the feet of Pope Clement as soon as the service was finished and said her husband was both blind and deaf, 'when he tried to pry into our affairs.'

Then Clement shed tears and urged all the people who were there to pray for Sisinnius that God would give him sight and hearing, and he went home with Theodora when their prayer had finished, and he had complete trust in Almighty God. And all Sisinnius's household stood weeping over him, and he could neither see nor hear when his household greeted Pope Clement and Theodora. Then Pope Clement raised up his eyes to the Lord and prayed for the Lord's grace for Sisinnius and spoke in this way:

'My Lord Jesus Christ, you who gave the keys of the Kingdom of Heaven to your Apostle Peter, my teacher and master, and you, holy God, said to him that everyone on earth shall be freed from all ills and obtain everlasting grace from God the Father through your holy intercession and a place in heaven when you wish to have it so, and everyone will be bound and condemned and become a fugitive from God when that is your verdict: now, Lord, command that the eyes and ears of this man be opened, for you have said thus: "Whatever you pray for, have faith, Christian men, that you will receive what you ask, and so shall it be (Matthew 21:22)."

En þetta heit þitt es víst satt ok hefir svá verit of allar veraldir veralda.'

En er allir svǫruþu þeir er hiá vǫru ok kvǫþu amen þá lukusk þegar
3   upp augu Sisinnius ok eyru.

En er Sisinnius sá Clemens páfa standa hiá konu sinni þá villtisk hugr
hans miǫk af mikilli illsku ok afbrýþi, ok ætlaþi svá firir sér at Clemens
6   páfi hefþi gervan hann mann blindan ok daufan af fiǫlkyngi sinni. En af
[œþi þeiri] ok heimsku es þá sló á hann Sisinnium, mælti hann viþ
þræla sína at þeir skyldi taka Clemens páfa ok binda hann ok draga
9   hann of ǫll stræti firir þá sǫk es hann fífldi konu hans ok tók sýn ok
heyrn frá honum meþ fiǫlkyngi sinni, sagþi Sisinnius. En þá þóttusk
þrælar hans draga Clemens páfa aptr ok fram at strætum sicut Sisinnius
12   bauþ þeim, herri þeira. En þar hlífþi Guþ heilagr Clemens páfa ástvin
sínum, ok drógu þeir eptir sér of stræti stokka ok steina. Ok svá sýndisk
Sisinnio sem þrælum hans at þeir drœgi þar Clemens páfa. En þeir inir
15   sǫmu hlœgismenn es eigi vissu hvat þeir gerþu ok hlógu svá at honum
sem at bandingia. En Sisinnius kvazk bana skyldu honum sem galdramǫnnum.

18   'Makliga dragiþ ér nú stokka ok steina,' sagþi Clemens páfi, 'þvíat ér
hafiþ steinhiǫrtu ok trúiþ á stokka ok steina.'

Þá veitti Clemens páfi blezun Theodoru ok fór heim síþan ok mælti
21   svá viþ hana at hon læti eigi af bœn sinni áþr Guþ heilagr miskunnaþi
Sisinnio búanda hennar. Ok þá vitraþisk henni Theodoru es hon var á
bœn sinni grátandi einn hverr gamall maþr gǫfugligr miǫk at áliti ok
24   sagþi henni svá:

'Firir bœnir þínar ok gœzku mun búandi þinn hiálpask, at þat sýnisk
es Póll bróþir minn dixit, "Helgask mun ótrúr maþr ok vándr af konu
27   sinni góþri ok trúri, ok vǫnd kona mun batna af sínum manni góþum ok
ráþvǫndum."'

En þá hvarf Pétr postoli braut frá henni. En Sisinnius kallaþi þegar á
30   konu sína Theodoru es hann sá hana, at þat sannaþisk es Pétr postoli
hafþi sagt henni, sicut vǫn var at honum:

'Biþþu nú Dominum Deum tuum at hann biargi mér, þóat ek siá óverþr,
33   af sinni heilagri miskunn ok sé mér eigi reiþr, þvíat afbrýþis sǫkum gekk
ek eptir þér í kirkiu inn, ok tók ek þegar víti á mér þá er ek forvitnuþumk
of þat at siá þá hluti ok heyra es gerþusk í návistu Clemens páfa. Nú
36   biþþu hann, þóat ek siá þess ómakligr, at hann komi til fundar viþ mik ok

7 *words supplied from Unger's edition*

And this your promise is certainly true and has been so through all ages of the world.'

And when all the people who were present answered and said Amen then Sisinnius's eyes and ears were immediately opened.

And when Sisinnius saw Pope Clement standing beside his wife, then his mind was much bewildered by intense malice and jealousy, and he thought to himself that Pope Clement had made him a blind and deaf man through his sorcery. And because of the madness and folly which then came over Sisinnius, he told his slaves that they should seize Pope Clement and bind him and drag him through all the streets because he had seduced his wife and taken his sight and hearing from him by his sorcery, said Sisinnius. And then his slaves thought that they were dragging Pope Clement back and forth through the streets as their master Sisinnius ordered them. But now Holy God protected his dear friend Pope Clement, and they were dragging stocks and stones behind them through the streets. And so it seemed to Sisinnius as it did to his slaves that they were dragging Pope Clement along there. But those same mockers who knew not what they were doing also laughed at him as if at a captive. And Sisinnius said that he would be put to death just like magicians.

'Fittingly do you now pull stocks and stones,' said Pope Clement, 'because you have hearts of stone and believe in stocks and stones.'

Then Pope Clement gave his blessing to Theodora and afterwards went home and told her that she should not cease her prayer until Holy God showed grace to her husband Sisinnius. And when she was at her prayers in tears a certain old man very noble in countenance appeared to Theodora and said to her:

'On account of your prayers and goodness your husband will be saved, so that it may be demonstrated as my brother Paul said: "A faithless and wicked man shall be sanctified by his good and faithful wife, and a wicked woman shall be made better through her good and upright husband (1 Corinthians 7:14)."'

And then the Apostle Peter disappeared from her. And Sisinnius called to his wife Theodora as soon as he saw her, so that what the Apostle Peter had told her became true, as was to be expected from him:

'Now ask the Lord your God that He may save me, though I am unworthy, by His holy grace, and not be angry with me, for it was because of jealousy I went after you into the church, and I was forthwith punished when I became desirous to see and hear the things that went on in Pope Clement's presence. Now beg him, though I do not deserve it, to come to see me and that I may know the true faith, for it

mega ek vita sanna trú, þvíat mér sýndisk svá ok þrælum mínum sem
vér byndim páfann siálfan þá er vér drógum stokka ok steina eptir oss.'

3 Þá fór Th⟨e⟩odora skyndiliga eptir Clemens páfa ok dixit honum
feginsamliga vitrun þessa ok tíþendi es Pétr postoli hafþi sýnzk henni,
ok hún dixit [feginsǫgu þ]ar meþ at Sisinnius mǫndi snúask frá villu
6 sinni sicut þegar gekk eptir, 'ok sendi hann mik nú eptir þér at þú skyldir
koma þangat til fundar hans.'
En Clemens dvalþi þá eigi ok fór feginn meþ henni. En Sisinnius tók
9 þá vegsamliga viþ honum sem makligt var es hann kom þingat. Clemens
páfi talþi þá firir honum trú rétta ok sanna ok hvat til andarheilsu skyldi
vinna. En Sisinnius tók þá at styrkiask í trú réttri, ok fell hann til fóta
12 Clemen⟨s⟩ páfa ok mælti síþan svá:
'Þakkir gerek nú sǫnnum Guþi,' dixit Sisinnius, 'ok almáttkum þeim es
mik lét blindan verþa ok daufan firir ótrú mína til þess at ek mega nú siá it
15 sanna ok heyra in réttu boþorþ þau er ek hafþa fyrr at skaupi haft. Ok es nú
hreinsat hugskot mitt frá ǫllum sauri skurþgoþavillu, þvíat þat es diǫfla
leyni ok fylskni þeira skurþgoþ þau er vér trúþum miǫk ok heimsliga á
18 hingat til, ok gǫfguþum af allri alúþ es verr var. En þau tæla alla þá menn
es þeim trúa. En ek skal nú trúa á Iesum Christum sannan Guþ á himnum.'
Þá fǫgnuþu allir kristnir menn es hugr hans skyldi svá vel skipazk
21 hafa á lítilli stundu. En Sisinnius tók þá skírn ok hiú hans vǫru skírþ at
páskum. En þar var allt saman sextán mǫnnum færa en þrettán þusundir.
Ok siá Sisinnius sneri síþan mǫrgum gǫfgum mǫnnum til réttrar trú af
24 orþum sínum ok góþum firirtǫlum, ok þeim iarteinum es hann hafþi af
Guþi þegnar ok af hans miskunn ok af kenningum Clemens páfa.
Þá reiddisk blótmaþr sá er Publius Torquatianus heitir viþ þat at hann
27 sá ótal manna snúask frá skurþgoþablótum ok til átrúnaþar viþ eingetinn
son Guþs Dominum nostrum Iesum Christum. Publius bar fé mikil á
ríkismenn víþa í heruþum ok baþ þá gera ófriþ mikinn kristnum mǫnnum.
30 Ok þá gerþusk þrætur miklar ok sundrþyki meþ Rúmaborgar lýþ of
Clemens páfa, ok gekk liþit sveitum miǫk ok mæltu sumir menn svá:
'Hvat hefir siá inn góþi Guþs vinr Clemens illa gert eþa hvat sé þat
33 góþra verka es eigi geri siá Guþs elskari ok ferr hverr maþr feginn frá
hans fundi þótt hryggr komi til hans. Ok siúkir menn fara heilir frá
Clemens páfa þeir es hans ástróþ sœkia ok hafa síþan, ok taka þar bæþi

5 *word and letter supplied by Unger*   22 þars

seemed to me and to my slaves too that we had bound the Pope himself when we were dragging stocks and stones behind us.'

Then Theodora hurried for Pope Clement and joyfully told him this revelation and tidings when the Apostle Peter had appeared to her, and she related the glad news also that Sisinnius would turn from his false belief, as was immediately fulfilled, 'and he has now sent me for you that you should come to see him there.'

And Clement did not delay and accompanied her joyfully. And Sisinnius then received him honourably as was fitting when he came there. Pope Clement explained to him about the correct and true faith and what he must do for his soul's welfare. And Sisinnius then began to grow strong in the true faith, and he fell at Pope Clement's feet, and then said as follows:

'I now give thanks to the true and almighty God,' said Sisinnius, 'who made me become blind and deaf on account of my unbelief so that I can now see the truth and hear the right commandments which I had previously mocked. Now my mind is purged of all the filth of idolatry, because these are the hiding places of devils and their secret dens: the idols which we hitherto believed in greatly and foolishly and worshipped with all earnestness, which was worse. But they entrap all people who believe in them. And I shall now believe in Jesus Christ the true God in heaven.'

Then all the Christians rejoiced that his mind should have changed so much for the better in a short time. And Sisinnius then received baptism and his household was baptised at Easter. And there were altogether sixteen people fewer than thirteen thousand there. And this Sisinnius afterwards converted many men of rank to the true faith by his words and effective persuasion, and by the signs which he had received from God and from His grace and from the teachings of Pope Clement.

Then a heathen worshipper who was called Publius Torquatianus grew angry when he saw a countless number of people turn from idolatrous sacrifice and to belief in the only begotten Son of God our Lord Jesus Christ. Publius bribed with many valuable gifts men in authority far and wide in the localities and told them to make all-out war on Christians. And then serious quarrels and discord arose among the people of Rome about Pope Clement and people were all divided into parties and some men spoke in this way:

'What has that good friend of God Clement done wrong or what kind of good deeds are there that this lover of God does not do?—and everyone goes from seeing him rejoicing, even though he came to him sad. And sick men leave Pope Clement healed who seek his friendly advice and afterwards take it, and there gain health in both soul and body. He does no heilsu andar ok líkama. Engum gerir hann grand né geig, en hann dugir ǫllum þeim es hans ráþ elska ok farsælisk hverr maþr af honum.'

3 Aþrir sveitarmenn svǫruþu ok sǫgþu svá:
'Af fiǫlkyngi einni gerir hann slíkt allt ok eyþir hann blót ór ok allri dýrþ goþa várra, ok ósœmir hann svá in gǫfgu [goþ ór at] hann segir at
6 Þórr sé eigi goþ, fulltrúi várr ok inn sterksti áss áræþisfullr, ok er nær hvars sem hann es blótinn. En þá ósœmþ ok óvirþing veitir hann Óþni órlausnafullum ok hvarfsemi at siá Clemens kallar hann fiánda ok
9 óhreinan anda. En hann kveþr Freyiu portkonu verit hafa, fœlir hann Frey, en hrœpir Heimdall, lastar hann Loka meþ slœgþ sína ok vélar ok kallar hann ok illan, hatar hann Hœni, bǫlvar hann Baldri, tefr hann Tý,
12 níþir hann Niǫrþ, illan segir hann Ull, flimtir hann Frigg, en hann geyr Gefiun, sekia dœmir hann Sif. Fir illsku sína kveþr hann svát orþi. Ok siá lagabriótr fœlir ǫll goþ ór ok lastar þau miǫk ok gremr at oss, ok
15 engi þeira ása má hann heyra vel látinn, hvártki Þór né Óþin. Ǫllum bindr hann þeim iamnan skiǫld upp goþum órum ok kallar ǫll óhœf meþ ǫllu, eþa hvárt heyrþu þér mann slíkt mæla fyrr? Blóti hann nú
18 þegar í staþ eþa hafi bana ella. Nú er sá dómr várr allra of hann.'

VIII

Þá lét Mamertus Iulianus Rúmarborgar greifi leiþa Clemens páfa leyniliga til máls viþ sik ok tók svá til orþa at 'allr Rúmaborgar lýþr
21 segir þig lasta miǫk goþ ór ok vera mann fiǫlkungan ok véldan miǫk af villu þeiri es þú gǫfgar Christum nekkvern, ókunnan mér, ok tekr þú upp nýbreytni þá í gegn goþum órum ok í mót lǫgum órum. Nú leggþu
24 niþr óskil þín ǫll ok dýrka in gǫfgu goþ ór.'

Sanctus Clemens svaraþi vel ok hófsamliga orþum greifans:
'Þess œski ek þér af tign þinni at þú megir ⟨skilia⟩ skynsemi rétta ok
27 rœþþu heldr viþ mik of skynsemismál en of þrætur ókunna manna ok heimskra. Þræta ok sundrþyki allt hefsk ávalt af ógegnum mǫnnum ok heimskum, ok má eigi til sanns ne eitt of fœra viþ þá. En í hlióþi skal
30 spakr maþr ok vitr spyria ok hyggia þá at heilsu sinni, ok leita meþ skynsemi hugar þíns ins sanna Guþs þess es þú mátt allt traust viþ hafa.'

5 *words supplied by Unger*   26 *word supplied by Larsson*

harm or injury to anyone, but he helps all those who value his counsel and everyone gets prosperity from him.'

Men of another party answered and said thus:

'He does all these things only by sorcery and he does away with our sacrifices and all the worship of our gods, and he dishonours our noble gods by saying that Þórr is not a god, our trusty patron and the strongest divinity, full of courage, and who is close at hand wherever he is worshipped. And he does this disgrace and dishonour to Óðinn who is always able to provide solutions and safety, that this Clement calls him a fiend and unclean spirit. And he declares that Freyja has been a harlot, he derides Freyr and slanders Heimdallr, he speaks ill of Loki and his cunning and tricks and says that he too is evil, he hates Hœnir, he curses Baldr, he hinders Týr, he libels Njǫrðr, he says that Ullr is evil, he ridicules Frigg, and he blasphemes Gefjun, he condemns Sif. He says these things because of his wickedness. And this law-breaker mocks all our gods and speaks much ill of them and makes them angry with us, and he cannot hear any of the gods spoken well of, neither Þórr nor Óðinn. He hangs up a similar shield* for each of these gods of ours and declares that they are all quite useless, but have you heard a man say such things before? Let him now sacrifice at once or else meet death. That is now the judgement of all of us on him.'

VIII

Then Mamertus Julianus, prefect of Rome, had Pope Clement brought in secret to speak with him and began to speak in this way, that 'all the people of Rome say that you speak much ill of our gods and that you are a man who is skilled in sorcery, and greatly deluded by false belief in that you worship a certain Christ, who is unknown to me, and you take up that new religion in defiance of our gods and contrary to our laws. Now abandon all your wrongful deeds and worship our noble gods.'

Blessed Clement answered the prefect's words politely and moderately: 'I wish this for you for the sake of your high rank that you may understand true wisdom and rather discuss rational matters with me than the disputes of ignorant and foolish people. All quarrelling and discord always originates from unreasonable and foolish people, and it is impossible to get them to see the truth of anything. But a wise and intelligent man must make quiet enquiry and then think of his salvation, and with your mind's understanding seek the true God on whom you can place complete trust.'

* This perhaps means that Clement hangs up a shield as a sign of his own ideals, as a mark of the gods' baseness, or as a challenge. There is no equivalent in either *Epitome de Gestis S. Petri* or *Martyrium S. Clementis* (*PG* 2).

Þá sendi Publius Torquatianus, eptir viþrmæli þessi þeira Clemens ok Iulianus greifa, rit ok innsigli meþ sendimǫnnum sínum til Traiano

3 keisera ok dixit svá at 'mikit su[n]drþyki gerisk meþ Rúmaborgar mǫnnum af kenningum Clemens páfa, ok spenr hann allt fólk ok allan landher frá allri dýrþ goþa várra ok dregr í villu sína ok til átrúnaþar viþ

6 Christum nekkvern, ok hann slæsk á it mesta ámæli viþ Þór eþa Óþin ok alla fœlir hann þá æsi ok ǫll goþ ór.'

En Traianus keiseri sendi þau orþ at móti at Clemens skyldi blóta

9 goþum þeira meþ sœmþ fullri eþa fara á braut ella ýr Rúmaborg of sæ nekkvern til útlegþar ok í eyþimǫrk. En Clemens páfi var heldr fúss til útlegþar ok meinlæta en hann hræddisk viþ, þvíat af ǫst þeiri heilagri es

12 hann unni almáttkum Guþi skein svá biart himinríkis sól í hiarta hans at hann var fúss til allra meinlæta þeira es Guþ heilagr vildi láta at hendi honum koma, þvíat hann vissi víst at Guþs miskunn mǫndi ávalt meþ

15 honum vera í hverri mannraun ok þraut. En þá tók Clemens ok talþi meþ góþum vilia trú rétta ok sanna firir greifanum svát hann komsk viþ miǫk of síþir greifinn ok felldi tǫr ákafliga ok mælti svá viþ Clemens,

18 þvíat Guþs mildi tœþi ávalt mǫlum páfans:

'Guþ þinn,' kvaþ greifinn, 'sá er þú trúir á af ǫllum hug ok gǫfgar vel ok trúliga ok dýrkar miǫk í ǫllu lífi þínu ok athæfi, veri hann ávalt meþ

21 þér ok efli hann þik til allra hluta ok farar þessar ok útlegþar.'

Ok gaf greifinn honum skip gott ok þá reiþu alla es honum var mest þǫrf at hafa meþ sér til ífarar þeirar ok baþ hann fara í miskunnarfri[þi]

24 Guþs síns þess er hann trúþi á. En heiþnir menn mǫttu eigi vatni halda es Clemens páfi skyldi skiliask viþ þá. Svá var hann ǫllum mǫnnum hugþekr ok ástfólginn miǫk at hvert barn unni honum.

27 En síþan skipaþi Clemens skip þat es greifinn hafþi gefit honum. En honum varþ liþ auþfengt til farar meþ sér, sem vǫn var at, þvíat margir kristnir menn vildu giarna honum fylgia, sem þeir gerþu. Ok fórsk þeim allt

30 it greizta unz þeir kómu í þann staþ es Certona heitir. En þar var liþ mikit firir meirr en tuttugu hundruþ kristinna manna ok í ánauþ þeiri at þeir telgþu griót, ok vǫru því þiáþir svá miǫk at þeir trúþu á Iesum Christum.

33 En er Clemens páfi vissi þat at þeir vǫru af því landflótta ok útlagir gervir at þeir vildu eigi hafna ǫst viþ Christum Dominum ok trú réttri, þá huggaþi Clemens þá meþ kenningum sínum ok mælti svá viþ þá alla saman:

36 'Makliga lét Christus Dominus meus mik hingat fara til yþvar at ek taka huggun meþ yþr af Guþi firir ór meinlæti.'

Then Publius Torquatianus sent, after this conversation between Clement and the prefect Julianus, letters and a seal by his messengers to the Emperor Trajan and said thus, that 'much discord arises among the people of Rome as a result of Pope Clement's teaching, and he is enticing all the population and all the people of the country away from all worship of our gods and draws them into his false doctrine and to belief in a certain Christ. And he has entered into the greatest abuse of Þórr and Óðinn and he mocks all the divinities and all our gods.'

And the Emperor Trajan sent these words in reply that Clement should sacrifice to their gods with full honour or else go away from Rome across some sea into exile and into the wilderness. But Pope Clement was more eager for exile and hardship than afraid of them, because through the sacred love which he had for almighty God, the sun of the Kingdom of Heaven shone so brightly in his heart that he was eager for all afflictions which Holy God wished to befall him, for he knew for certain that God's grace would always be with him in every trial and labour. And then Clement went and declared with good will the right and true faith to the prefect so that the prefect was in the end deeply moved and shed tears fervently and said thus to Clement, for God's grace always assisted the Pope's words:

'Your God,' said the prefect, 'whom you believe in with all your mind and worship well and faithfully and glorify greatly in all your life and works, may he always be with you and strengthen you for all things and for this journey and exile.'

And the prefect gave him a good ship and all the equipment which he would most need to have with him on this journey and told him to go in the peace and grace of his God in whom he believed. But the heathens could not hold back their tears when Pope Clement had to leave them. So endeared was he to all people and well beloved that every child was fond of him.

And then Clement got a crew for the ship which the prefect had given him. And it was easy for him to get people to go with him, as was to be expected, for many Christians were eager to accompany him, which they did. And their journey went extremely well until they reached the place which is called Certona. And a large host was there before them, more than two thousand Christian people, and employed as slaves to cut stones, and they were so harshly enslaved because they believed in Jesus Christ. And when Pope Clement knew that they had been exiled and banished because they would not abandon their love for the Lord Christ and the true faith, then Clement comforted them with his teaching and said thus to all of them together:

'It is fitting that my Lord Christ allowed me to come hither to you that I may take comfort with you from God for our hardships.'

En þeir sǫgþu honum til sinna vandræþa at þeir urþu sex mílur allar
at bera vatn á baki sér, 'þvíat eigi getr nærr svá,' sǫgþu þeir.

3   'Biþium vér nú allir saman,' dixit Clemens páfi, 'at Dominus noster
Iesus Christus lúki upp brunn góþan firir iáterum sínum, sá er forþum
gaf Moisi vatn ór steini ok lýþ sínum í eyþimǫrk, svát vér megim nú
6   fagna góþum giǫfum hans ok iarteinum, þvíat hann mon veita oss
miskunn sem ǫllum es hann biþia nauþsynligra hluta meþ ástsamri trú.'

En þá er þeir hǫfþu lokit bœn sinni þá litaþisk Clemens umb ok sá
9   hann lamb standa til hœgri handar sér á hóli einum, ok rétti lambit fót
sinn ok tafsaþi honum, sicut þar væri vaz vǫn undir. Ok þá skilþi Clemens
af krapti Heilags Anda at Guþ omnipotens sýndi honum einum lamb
12   þat. En hann varþ þessi miskunn Guþs ok sýn feginn miǫk ok fór hann
þegar þangat sem Guþ sýndi honum sitt tákn ok mælti svá viþ kristna
menn, at 'í þessum staþ grafiþ ér nú iǫrþina in nomine Patris ok Sonar
15   ok Anda Heilags.'

En er þeir grófu þar iǫrþina miǫk langa stund ok fundu eigi þann staþ
es lambit hafþi tafsat, til þess at omnipotens Guþ birti þat enn framarr
18   ok berligarr hversu miklu hæstan verþleik siá inn miskunnsamasti
Clemens páfi hafþi viþ Guþ á himnum, þá tók Clemen⟨s⟩ páfi graftól í
hǫnd sér ok hió tysvar pálinum niþr undir fœtr lambinu. En þar spratt
21   þegar mikil ǫ́ upp ok fór rennandi, þvíat Guþ dvalþi eigi miskunn sína
þegar es þær inar helgu hendr ok inar lítillátu æstu Guþ giafar miskunn-
samligrar viþ sik. Ok lýsti Guþ ifir því at af krapti ok verþleik ins helga
24   Clemens veitti hann mesta þessa ina dásamligstu ástgiǫf viþ fólkit. Þá
urþu þeir allir fegnir iartein þessi es Guþ hafþi þeim veitta firir trú rétta,
ok sungu þeir hótt lof Guþi almáttkum ok mæltu svá at 'rennandi ǫ́
27   gleþr borg Guþs'. Ok þá drifu margir heraþsmenn þingat es þeir frágu
iarteinir þessar ok þeir sǫ́ þessa ǫ́ renna ok upp spretta þar er þeir hǫfþu
ávalt vitat fyrr þurran staþ. En þeim brá miǫk viþ þessi tíþendi ok vel es
30   þeir knáttu þar líta. En meþ því at Guþ heilagr unni þeim mǫnnum mikillar
farsælu sicut ǫllum ǫþrum þeim es meþ góþfýsi sóttu á fund Clemens
páfa, þvíat af hans orþum fýstisk siá allr mannabólkr [til lifanda Guþs]
33   es slíkar vingiafar gefr ok veitir af sinni heilagri miskunn, [tó]ku þar trú
ok skírn á þeim degi meirr *en* fimm hundruþ manna. Ok svá vel efldisk
þar kristinn dómr at á þeim misserum var hálfr átti tøgr kirkna þar gǫrr

And they told him their troubles, that they were forced to carry water on their backs for six miles in all, 'because there is none to be had closer,' they said.

'Let us now all pray together,' said Pope Clement, 'that our Lord Jesus Christ, who once gave water out of rock to Moses and his people in the wilderness, will open up a good spring for his confessors, so that we may now rejoice in his good gifts and miracles, for he will grant us grace, as to all who pray to him for necessary things with loving faith.'

And when they had finished their prayer, then Clement looked around and he saw a lamb standing to his right on a hillock, and the lamb stretched out its leg and tapped it, as if there were hope of finding water beneath it. And then Clement understood from the power of the Holy Ghost that Almighty God was revealing the lamb to him alone. And he was very joyful at this act of God's grace and this vision and he went at once to the place where God revealed his sign to him and said thus to the Christians that 'you must now dig the earth in this place in the name of Father and Son and Holy Ghost.'

And when they had dug the earth there for a very long time and had not found the place where the lamb had tapped, so that Almighty God might display still further and more clearly by how much this most compassionate Pope Clement had the highest merit in the eyes of God in heaven, then Pope Clement took a spade in his hand and dug the spade in twice under the feet of the lamb. And straightaway a great stream sprang up and went flowing there, for God did not delay his grace once those holy and humble hands had desired a gift of grace from him. And God made it known that it was mostly because of the power and merit of the Blessed Clement that he was giving this most marvellous gift of love to the people. Then they all rejoiced at this miracle that God had granted to them for their true faith, and they sang high praise to Almighty God and said thus that 'a flowing river gladdens the city of God' (Psalm 46:4 [45:5]). And then many men of the district thronged there when they heard of these miracles and they saw this river flowing and springing up there where they had previously always found a dry place. And they were amazed when they heard what had happened and delighted when they were able to see it. And because Holy God granted those men good fortune as he did to everyone else who went to see Pope Clement with good will, since through his words this entire host of men became desirous for the living God, who gives and bestows such gifts of friendship through his holy grace, more than five hundred men received Faith and baptism on that day. And the Christian faith prospered so well there that in that year

ok vígþar af kennimǫnnum, ok svá ǫll skurþgoþ brotin í þeim heruþum
ok ǫll hof eydd ok allir blótstallar brenndir. Ok þá hlógu kristnir menn at
3 ótru heiþinna manna ok blótum þeira.

En því næst kom sú saga firir Traianum keisera at ótal manna snerisk
til Christi frá blótum af kenningu Clemens páfa. Ok þá var dómandi sá
6 sendr þingat af hendi konung⟨s⟩ins es Aufidianus hét til þess at pína ok
vega marga kristna menn. En er greifinn fann þat ok reyndi at þeir vǫru
allir fúsir inir kristnu menn til písla ok bana firir Guþs sakar þá vægþi
9 hann mannfiǫlþa þeim ok lét taka Clemens einn saman, en hann neyddi
aþra til blóta sem hann mátti mest. En er hann sá hug Clemens páfa
staþfastan í trú heilagri ok á þiónustu viþ Guþ á himnum, þá mælti hann
12 viþ þióna sína ok þræla at þeir skyldi feria Clemens páfa út á sió langt
frá landi ok binda mikit akkeri viþ háls honum ok søkkva honum svá
niþr í sióvardiúp at eigi taki kris⟨t⟩nir menn at gǫfga hann sem goþ. En
15 síþan gripu þeir Gyþingar inn gǫfga Clemens páfa ok rǫru út frá landi
miǫk langt. En síþan lǫgþu þeir hendr á Clemens ok bundu akkeri viþ
háls honum ok skutu þeim inum staþrama Guþs kappa útan borz, ok
18 galt hann svá þá ina helgu ǫnd Guþi es fylgt hafþi þeim inum hreina
líkama es þeir hǫfþu þá firir borþ lagþan.

En þá stóþu allir kristnir menn á sævarstrǫndu grátandi eptir es þeir
21 fœrþu Clemens páfa til bana, ok vóru í inni mestu sorgmœþi hugar síns
es þeira ástvinr var tekinn ok numinn ór hǫndum þeim til meinlætis ok
ógurligs bana allt til þess unz lærisveinar hans Febus ok Cornelius
24 hugguþu lýþinn ok mæltu svá:

'Biþium vér allir brœþr meþ einfǫldum hug,' kvóþu þeir, 'at Dominus
noster Iesus Christus sýni oss píningarvátt sinn Clemens páfa.'

27 Ok fellu þeir þar allir til iarþar ok bóþu lítillátliga Guþ at þeir knætti
siá líkama ins sæla Clemens páfa. En þá gerþusk þær iarteinir inar
hvarmiklu at særinn fell út frá landi of þriár mílur, ok þá gengu kristnir
30 þar eptir meþ lofi ins hæsta Guþs. Ok veitti Guþ heilagr lýþ sínum þurra
gǫtu unz þeir kómu at musteri miklu ok ítarligu harþla þvíat englar
Guþs hǫfþu gert ýr marmaragrióti. Þeir gengu inn í musteri þat ok
33 dýrkuþu þann Guþ es þeim veitti [þat] firir verþleik ok dýrþ sanna
Clemens páfa ok firir bœnir hans lærisveina at þ[eir] fundu þar líkama
Clemens páfa, ok lagþan í nýia steinþró ok akkeri þar hiá honum lagit

---

6 Ausidianus   33–34 words supplied by Unger

seventy-five churches were built there and consecrated by clerics, and also all idols were broken up in those localities and all temples destroyed and all heathen altars burnt. And then Christian men laughed at the unbelief of heathens and their worship.

And next the story reached the Emperor Trajan that countless people were turning to Christ from heathen rites as a result of Pope Clement's teaching. And then a judge who was called Aufidianus was sent there on behalf of the king in order to torture and kill many Christians. And when the prefect discovered and learnt from experience that all the Christians were ready to suffer torture and death for the sake of God, then he spared the multitude and had Clement alone seized, and he compelled others to sacrifice as best he could. And when he saw Pope Clement's mind was steadfast in the holy Faith and in the service of God in heaven, then he instructed his servants and slaves that they should carry Pope Clement out to sea far from land and tie a large anchor to his neck and sink him down into the depths of the sea so that Christians should not begin to worship him as a god. And then the Jews seized the noble Pope Clement and rowed out very far away from land. And then they laid hands on Clement and tied an anchor to his neck and threw the steadfast champion of God overboard, and so he yielded up to God the holy soul which had belonged to the pure body which they had then thrown overboard.

And then all the Christians stood behind on the sea-shore weeping when they took Pope Clement to his death, and were in the greatest distress of mind when their beloved friend was seized and taken out of their hands to the anguish of an awful death right until his disciples Febus and Cornelius comforted the people and said thus:

'Let all of us brothers pray with a single mind,' they said, 'that our Lord Jesus Christ may show us his martyr Pope Clement.'

And they all fell to the earth there and humbly asked God that they might see the body of the Blessed Pope Clement. And then the very great miracles took place that the sea receded three miles from the land, and then Christians walked out after it with praise of the highest God. And Holy God gave his people a dry path until they came to a large and very splendid temple which God's angels had built of marble. They went inside the temple and worshipped the God who granted them on account of the merit and true glory of Pope Clement and on account of the prayers of his disciples that they might find there the body of Pope Clement, and placed in a new stone coffin and an anchor laid down there beside him next to the

niþr hiá altari. Ok þær rúnar fundusk á steinþró páfans at þeir tœki hann
eigi á braut þaþan, því at svá myklu mest dýrþ ⟨var⟩ þessum inum ítarliga
3 Guþs vin veitt at greftri ok at þiónustu sanctorum engla almáttigs Guþs
sem nú má heyra. Ok þær iarteinir gerask þar á hveriu ári of hótíþ
Clemens páfa at sær fellr út af landi ok veitir Guþ heilagr þar þurra gǫtu
6 at ganga til Clemens viku alla í samt. Firir verþleik Clemens gefr Guþ
þá miskunn mǫnnum til hiálpar sér at þeir dýrki þar Guþ í þeim staþ ok
inn helga Clemens páfa.

9 En þá er menn hǫfþu lokit bœn sinni þar, þá létu menn aptr vannliga
kirkiudyrr eptir sér ok fór hverr heim á leiþ til síns herbergis. En sær
fell at landi hvínanda ok haf kolblátt meþ ǫllu eptir œþi sínu. En faþir
12 sveinsins þess es somnaþr var í Clemenskirkiu þá er aþrir menn fóru á
braut þaþan ok móþir hans leituþu sonar síns á meþal kuþra manna
sinna ok kunningia, þvíat þau sǫknuþu hans eigi fyrr en þá es þau vǫru
15 heim á fǫr komin, ok vættu þess ok vilnuþusk at hann mǿndi fylgt hafa
nágrǫnnum þeira. En þau fundu hann eigi sem glíkligt var, þvíat
sveinninn svaf fast eptir í musterinu þá er annat liþ fór á braut þaþan.
18 En faþir sveinsins ok móþir urþu harþla dǫpr viþ tión sonar síns ok
ætluþu þau þat firir sér at sær mǿndi sveininum hafa grandat í útanfǫr
þeira, ok sǫkuþu sik of glœp sinn ok athugaleysi es þau hǫfþu eigi gáþ
21 sunar síns. En at iamlengþ annars vetrar Clemensdag siálfan þá fell sær
út frá landi at vanþa sínum ok gingu menn þurrum fótum til Clemenskirkiu. Ok kómu þau hiú þar fyrst til musteris allra manna es sonar síns
24 þóttusk misst hafa. En þau urþu þá fegin es sonr þeira var lífs í Clemenskirkiu ok rann hann þegar á mót þeim meþ inum mesta fagnaþi ok inu
mesta ástríki viþ bæþi þau fǫþur sinn ok móþur. En þau spurþu son sinn
27 at því hversu hann of mætti svá lengi fœzlulaust of lifa þar . . .

12 es] + er

altar. And this writing was found on the Pope's stone coffin that they should not take him away from there, since by so much the greatest glory was granted to this splendid friend of God in his burial and in the service of holy angels of Almighty God as can now be heard. And these miracles take place there each year at the feast of Pope Clement that the sea flows out from the land and Holy God provides a dry path there all that week to walk to Clement's church. For the merit of Clement God gives this grace to men for their salvation that they may worship God and the holy Pope Clement there in that place.

And when men had finished their prayers there, then they carefully shut the church-doors after them, and each made his way back home to his dwelling. And the water and coal-black sea flowed hissing back to the land entirely in accordance with its nature. And the father of the boy who had fallen asleep in Clement's church when other people went away from there, and his mother, looked for their son among their friends and acquaintances, because they had not missed him until they were on their way home and expected and hoped that he would have gone with their neighbours. But naturally they did not find him, because the boy was fast asleep back in the temple when other people went away from there. And the boy's father and mother were very sad at the loss of their son and they imagined that the sea must have harmed the boy during their journey back, and they blamed themselves for their wickedness and carelessness in that they had not kept an eye on their son. And on the anniversary the following winter, on Clement's day itself, then the sea flowed out from the land as usual and people walked dry-shod to Clement's church. And the husband and wife who thought that they had lost their son arrived first at the temple before everyone else. And then they were joyful that their son was alive in Clement's church and he immediately ran towards them with the greatest joy and the greatest love for both his father and mother. And they asked their son about how he was able to survive there so long without food . . .*

---

* See Introduction, p. xix above.

INDEX